LEONARD WOOD
ON
NATIONAL ISSUES

From a drawing by Boardman Robinson

LEONARD WOOD

LEONARD WOOD

ON

NATIONAL ISSUES

The Many-Sided Mind of a Great Executive
Shown by His Public Utterances

COMPILED BY

EVAN J. DAVID

With a Foreword by Edward S. Van Zile

GARDEN CITY   NEW YORK
DOUBLEDAY, PAGE & COMPANY
1920

To

FREDERICK MOORE

A Friend and Fellow

of my own Craft

FOREWORD

WHATEVER may be the outcome of the Presidential contest of 1920, the fact has been well established that Major General Leonard Wood has won for himself a permanent place among the truly great Americans of this generation, and that his personality and achievements will be accorded attentive study by all historians who may endeavor to give to posterity an accurate account of our country's influence upon the destinies of mankind during the epoch-making first quarter of the twentieth century. In presenting to the public, therefore, the many-sided personality of Leonard Wood as revealed through his writings and speeches, Mr. David, the compiler of this timely volume, has been inspired by the belief that his work was not ephemeral, that there would be permanent value in a collection of this virile, versatile American's public utterances regarding the vital questions that agitate a period overwhelmed by the vast significance of the problems it is called upon to solve.

The cynic who asserted that speech was

vouchsafed to us that we might manage to conceal our thoughts must have associated with men of a type with which Leonard Wood has nothing in common. His clear thinking leads him irresistibly to clarity of expression, and his intrinsic sincerity, his romantically varied experiences of life, his supreme courage and the white heat of his patriotism combine to give to his views on the basic principles involved in our present national and international complications a significance that will outlast any connection they may seemingly have with the political activities of the moment.

Convinced, as the compiler is, that Leonard Wood's attitude toward the vital problems of our generation is an integral part of the history of our time, of import to the future as well as to the present, the endeavor has been made in the following pages to throw upon many vexed questions the illuminating light of this great leader's trained mind, a mind free from visionary tendencies, clear, logical, broadly sympathetic, and always American in its contact with contemporary issues.

The Standard Dictionary defines a statesman as "a man versed in the arts of government." To his mental and temperamental qualifications for statesmanship, Leonard Wood has added the illuminating experiences of an administrator in several parts of the world, an experience that has given to him an enviable reputation in his own country and among foreigners as one "versed in the arts of government." It required the forcefulness combined with tact of a thoroughly-equipped statesman to bring order out of chaos to Cuba, opportunity for advancement to the Philippines and law-enforcement without bloodshed to Gary, Ind.

In presenting to the public the following diversified evidences of Leonard Wood's masterly grasp of the great problems of our generation, Mr. David wishes to express his thanks for courtesies extended to him by the *Outlook,* the *Metropolitan Magazine,* the *Ladies' Home Journal,* P. F. Collier & Son, Reilly and Britton and Mr. F. L. Huidekoper.

In conclusion, permit me to say that my knowledge regarding the career of the compiler increases the pleasure I have taken in writing this foreword. Mr. David's early career was spent in manual labor in coal mines. Ambitious and courageous, he worked his way through Harvard University, and has, through

industry and ability, become a writer of books
and magazine articles. The broad sympathies
that his varied contacts with life have given
him naturally make of him an enthusiastic ad-
mirer of Leonard Wood, who also worked his
way through Harvard University and is, like
Mr. David, a many-sided lover of his kind.

EDWARD S. VAN ZILE.

CONTENTS

PAGE

Frontispiece

FOREWORD vii

INDEX xi

THE COMPILER'S INTRODUCTION . . . xiii

HOW CUBA WON SELF-DETERMINATION . . 3

CAPITAL, LABOR AND THE GOLDEN RULE . . 19

AMERICAN WOMEN—TODAY AND TOMORROW . 27

WAR AND PEACE 33

THE LEAGUE OF NATIONS 45

THE FARMER—HIS RIGHTS AND WRONGS . . 49

TEACHERS, MOULDERS OF THE FUTURE . . 59

IMMIGRATION WITHOUT ASSIMILATION . . 63

OUR DEFENSIVE WEAPONS 71

AMERICANIZATION 75

ARBITRATION—ITS VALUE AND LIMITATIONS . 83

NEEDED—SOUND MINDS IN SOUND BODIES . . 89

ORGANIZED GOOD SAMARITANS 97

NO PARLEY WITH THE REDS 103

OUR DUTY TO OUR VETERANS . . . 109

SOLDIERS AS LIFE-SAVERS 115

OUR PROGRAM IN A NUTSHELL . . . 121

GROVER CLEVELAND 123

THEODORE ROOSEVELT 125

I

IN COMPILING this book the object has been to collect representative statements from the speeches and writings of General Leonard Wood on national problems. At first the idea was to confine the volume to selections from Wood's recent speeches and writings which touch on present-day affairs, but on investigation it was soon discovered that much else that Wood had said was well worth including.

While it is true that Wood has not been able to take the time to give exhaustive treatment to some topics which he has discussed, yet it is a fact that, in the brief statements which he has made, he has singled out the cardinal principles of the issues, and has clearly enunciated his position on each particular subject in hand, displaying his analytical method in arriving at conclusions. This is especially true of his speeches upon Americanization, the Reds, and Farm Problems.

In all his writings and speeches, Leonard Wood reveals his sterling patriotism, his clear vision and the high moral platform from

which he judges every issue. Always his point
of view seems to be the greatest good for the
greatest number; always he places his country
first. Always his sympathies are with the oppressed, the down-trodden and the unfortu-
nate. Always his statements are delivered
with the object of righteousness, uplift and
patriotism. His broad human sympathy can
be compared only with that of his friend, the
late Theodore Roosevelt.

II

GENERAL WOOD'S style, as revealed
in his speeches and writings, is best explained
in his own words when speaking of the style
of Roosevelt:

"In speech he was simple and direct. His
purpose was to go directly to the heart of his
subject in the simplest and clearest language;
he used words to convey ideas, never to be-
fuddle the public. . . . You know exactly what he means when you finish what he
has written; there are no empty phrases nor
glittering, unsound idealism, but just a plain
statement of those simple truths which are the
wisdom of the ages, the deductions of right
thinking men and women."

General Wood uses very few figures of speech. His language is the simple language of the Bible and Abraham Lincoln. His vocabulary consists largely of words derived from the Anglo-Saxon rather than from the Latin. He makes no attempt at the use of symbolism which may confuse, or convey a doubtful meaning. Practically no ornamentation is contained in the General's speeches or writings. When he does use a figure of speech, it is usually very clear and graphic, such as the one in which he compared Roosevelt to a boulder standing solid against the on-rushing waters, or when he complained that unrestricted immigration to America was putting too much sand into our concrete. Like General Grant in his autobiography, General Wood uses the speech and the language of the soldier; it is direct, forceful and clear, and is never employed for any other purpose than to drive home an argument. This gives a ruggedness and strength to the General's speeches and writings that remind one of the hills and mountains of his native New England, and reveal the eminently substantial, solid, determined, dignified character of the man. His words are full of sincerity, honesty and sterling integrity, such as we always associate with the character and writings of Abraham Lincoln.

III

IT MAY be said by some that the selections do not cover every question before the American public at the present time. That may be true, but the most important and vital ones are certainly treated very definitely and very clearly. In extenuation it can be said that Leonard Wood has been too busy of late with his multifarious duties as Commander of the Central Department—where so many of the great strikes and disorders occurred during the year 1919—to go on record on every subject. And he has also been hampered or restrained by the fact that as an officer in the army he could not at all times speak freely.

In regard to Internationalism, General Wood had written a great deal before we entered the war. How far his views have been modified by the Great War can be perceived by reading his more recent references to the subject. Extensive quotations from those writings show the reasons why he takes the stand that he does. Since the armistice he has also gone on record to the effect that he does not believe that the League of Nations will abolish war; and he states that the treaty should be adopted with the Lodge reservations.

In regard to his position on the Labor question, perhaps it ought to be stated here that General Wood, while at Gary, did not limit free speech, provided nothing hostile to our form of government was said and provided no words were uttered to incite the strikers to violate law and order. He allowed the strikers to meet in their halls and he granted Mr. John Fitzpatrick, leader of the steel workers' organization, the privilege of addressing the strikers in the public square after Mr. Fitzpatrick had given General Wood his word that nothing to incite disorder would be uttered. Mr. Fitzpatrick kept his word. General Wood also permitted pickets to be stationed by the strikers, but he would not allow them to intimidate any man or to coerce or interfere with any person who wished to go to work. The same thing was true in the coal fields of West Virginia. In this way, by his tact, General Wood prevented bloodshed and no property was destroyed during the time that his troops occupied those districts, nor was a single shot fired.

IV

ON THE matter of preparedness, General Wood believes that a small standing army of 225,000 men is sufficient, but he also believes that the physically fit young men of the land ought to have six months' intensive training in their nineteenth year.

The Reds and the I. W. Ws. General Wood has very vehemently denounced. To quote his own words, "There is no room for the red flag in this country," and "we should kill it as we would a snake." But while at times allowing himself such liberty of expression, he has also explained very carefully and definitely that any and all action against those who would destroy our government should be orderly and within the law.

No man in the country was better able to appreciate and analyze the character of Theodore Roosevelt than General Wood. This was due to their long and intimate friendship and to the fact that they had worked out so many problems together. This section of the work is illuminating, for it may be clearly seen that

Wood, in his analysis of the former President, has given an explanation of the underlying sentiments which Wood shared, and which have shaped his opinions and beliefs.

In urging Americanization, General Wood has touched upon the cardinal evils that now threaten the country and has suggested remedies.

General Wood's familiarity with educational problems in Cuba and his views on the importance of education as a means of Americanization and progress clearly show that the teachers who instruct our children should certainly be paid better if we hope to get the right kind of instructors to perform that important task.

v

LIKE Theodore Roosevelt, Leonard Wood knew the important part that women would play in the forming of the policies of the Nation in the future and gave expression to his views on this timely and vital subject.

In regard to the Farm Problems, Leonard Wood's extensive travels and keen observation in all sections of the United States together with the fact that he was brought up in a rural community make his views on agricultural subjects carry considerable weight.

Although this volume is not exhaustive, it contains much that should be inspiring to true Americans, and no matter how much we differ with General Wood in regard to the way in which certain problems should be solved, we cannot gainsay the fact that he is animated by sincerity and patriotism and that his sayings reveal the sterling honesty and integrity of the man. In the following pages General Wood will speak for himself, and there can be no doubt that the cumulative effect of his splendid and inspiring outpourings regarding the vital issues of the day will convince every open-minded reader that among the great Americans of our time there is none greater than Leonard Wood.

EVAN J. DAVID

LEONARD WOOD

ON

NATIONAL ISSUES

LEONARD WOOD ON NATIONAL ISSUES

How Cuba Won Self-Determination

I

THE purpose of our military government of Cuba, after the Spanish War, was to prepare the Cubans for self-government and to establish conditions which would render the establishment of a Cuban republic possible and its orderly and successful maintenance probable. The occupation of Cuba began with the occupation of the city of Santiago and extended rapidly over the province of the same name. The territory occupied by the military forces of the United States prior to the general transfer of the Island, January 1, 1899, was limited to this province. Conditions in Santiago at the time of occupancy were as unfavorable as can be imagined. Yellow fever, pernicious malaria and intestinal fevers were all prevalent to an alarming extent. The city

3

and surrounding country were full of sick
Spanish soldiers, starving Cubans and the
sick of their own army. The sanitary conditions were indescribably bad. There was little
or no water available and the conditions were
such as can be imagined to exist in a tropical
city following a siege and capture in the most
unhealthy season of the year.

The first work undertaken was feeding the
starving, taking care of the sick, cleaning up
and removing the dangerous material in the
city. In addition to correcting these local conditions, it was necessary to send food and
medicine throughout the province, maintain
order, re-establish municipal government, re-
organize the courts, and do the thousand and
one things incident to re-establishing the sem-
blance of government in a stricken and de-
moralized community. The actual difficulties
were increased by the fact that the people with
whom we had to deal spoke a foreign language
with which few of us were familiar. The death
rate among our own troops was heavy and the
percentage of sick appalling. The regulars
and volunteers engaged in the siege and capture of the city were withdrawn late in August
and their places filled with one regiment of

regulars and a number of regiments of volunteers. The arrival of these green troops in the height of the unhealthy season was a cause of grave anxiety and their care required unusual precautions. By this time the city had been cleaned; the death rate greatly checked; food had been sent by pack train to the interior and by sea to the various seaport towns of the province and couriers had been sent through the country to inform the inhabitants where they could procure food and medicine; custom houses had been established at all the ports and with the funds collected from this source public works had already been undertaken.

II

THE first public works were carried out in the city of Santiago to drain certain unhealthy surroundings of the city, improve the water supply and render the place more habitable. The purpose of the public works was not only to improve conditions, but to give occupation to the thousands of idle people, including disbanded soldiers of the Cuban army. Some were paid in money and some in rations. Every effort was made to get the people out to their homes in the country, and, with this in view, men were furnished with a few necessary agricultural implements and food enough for a month and sent out to their homes. In this way thousands of idle people about the city were disposed of and placed upon their own property, and surrounded with those members of their families who had survived the war and its consequences.

A rural guard composed of Cubans was rapidly organized for the maintenance of order in the rural districts. During this period troops were also used for this purpose. As soon as conditions of actual starvation had been done away with, and the worst features of the sanitary situation improved, steps were taken to organize municipal government in the various towns. There was no time to write an electoral law and put it in force. The method adopted was to go to a town, assemble from sixty to one hundred men representing all classes of the people and ask them to name municipal officers and to present their list as soon as completed. In this way the officials of all the municipalities of the province were in time appointed. Temporary regulations were drawn up governing local taxation. Stores and business houses were divided into classes and were required to pay so much per month to the municipal treasury. Under the means so procured, municipal governments were started. Expenses were kept at the lowest figure.

III

AS SOON as a municipal government was organized, steps were taken to temporarily relieve the situation in each municipality, and medicine, food and assistance were given those most needful of it. The next step was to establish village schools in all the different towns. In October the Spanish garrison, consisting of twelve thousand men, was withdrawn from the northwest portion of the province. Upon the withdrawal it was found that smallpox was epidemic in most of the towns that they had occupied and an investigation showed that there were approximately three thousand cases of smallpox existing in the Holguin district and that the disease was of a malignant type. Six hundred men of the 2d Immunes under Colonel Hood were vaccinated and re-vaccinated, under the careful supervision of their surgeons. When this was completed they were all sent into the infected districts accompanied by several extra medical officers and charged with the suppression of the epidemic, a work which was soon completed. Some twelve hundred cases of smallpox were treated in hospitals. Small settlements (made up as a rule of thatched houses), where it was most prevalent, were burned. Settlements containing buildings of permanent construction were thoroughly disinfected, and some thirty thousand people vaccinated. The efforts taken were effective in bringing the disease to a summary conclusion, and since this epidemic Cuba has been free from smallpox. As an illustration of the efficiency of vaccination, it can be stated that there was not a case of smallpox among troops sent into the districts.

IV

WITH the stamping out of this epidemic, the worst features of the sanitary situation were removed, and affairs began to have a more hopeful outlook, and at the end of the year the province was orderly and fairly healthy; municipal governments were running,

with rather crude machinery to be sure, but
performing the necessary functions. Nearly
two hundred public schools had been established, and all incurred expenses had been paid
from revenues collected, and approximately
$160,000 was on hand for carrying out certain
sanitary work in the city of Santiago, for
which arrangements had been made. The
Supreme Court, courts of first instance, for
municipal courts had been established throughout the province. Custom houses were in
operation, and starvation had disappeared. A
proclamation embodying the general principles of a Bill of Rights had been published,
giving the people the right to carry arms, to
hold public meetings, and, in fact, to do all
things which people do under free governments. Such was the condition in the province
of Santiago at the time of the transfer of the
island to the United States on January 1,
1899.

Conditions were encountered in Havana
similar to those in Santiago, but not so severe,
as the city had not undergone a siege and had
not suffered from the demoralizing conditions
necessarily following. Still the condition was
exceedingly grave and an immense amount of

work was required to place affairs upon a comparatively normal basis. The work of straightening out Havana, both in a sanitary and administrative sense, was performed with singular ability by General William Ludlow, since deceased. General Ludlow's work was of the highest character, and was carried out by the exercise of excellent judgment and great ability, and the work which he accomplished resulted in a saving of thousands of lives and in the organization of a suitable government in Havana and the establishment of good sanitary conditions. Similar work, and on a smaller scale, was carried out by General Wilson in Matanzas, General Carpenter in Puerto Principe, and other officers in various parts of the island.

v

THE work outside of Havana called for extensive care of country people in the way of supplying food, medicines, etc., and was carried out with remarkable ability by our officers. During the year 1899, under the administration of General Brooke and his subordinates, an organization of the courts in the four west-

ern provinces of the island was accomplished;
municipal governments were inaugurated; and
police forces provided for the rural districts.
A rudimentary school law had been published
and preparations were under way for the establishment of a school system. Custom
houses had been established, under the supervision of General Tasker H. Bliss, and
revenues were regularly collected.

This was the condition of affairs in Decem-
ber, 1899, at which time I was appointed Military Governor of the island. A year and a
half of experience in Cuba had shown that the
island was in need of a general revision of the
law of public works, beneficence, education,
municipal administration, prison administration, etc.; that it needed an electoral law; and,
in fact, that the whole machinery of the government needed overhauling and readjustment. The general law was excellent. I shall
always feel indebted to Justice White, of the
Supreme Court, for some very sensible advice
which he gave me to the effect that the law was
all right, but to look out for the procedure,
which needed many modifications. President
McKinley's instructions to me were to prepare
Cuba, as rapidly as possible, for the establish-

ment of an independent government, republican in form; to arrange for an efficient administration of justice; and a good school system. Whatever results were obtained were made possible by the policy of the President and the Secretary of War in defining the object to be attained and leaving their representative in the island to work it out, and he was given entire freedom in so doing.

VI

THE government was transferred eventually to the Cuban people exactly as promised, with no debts but, of course, some current liabilities for public works in process of construction, and with $1,613,000 free for allotment. Approximately 97 per cent. of the officials were Cubans, and they proved loyal and efficient and honest. The courts of justice were entirely in the hands of the people. The attitude of the Spanish element was always friendly. They represent the bulk of the business interests of the island. They are people of order, and make excellent citizens.

Cuba has been given an excellent start. What she needs now is the establishment of good economic relations with the United States; in other words, a reasonable degree of reciprocity. Her purchases have been in the neighborhood of $68,000,000 per year, and with confidence and stimulation to business which will come with reciprocity, we shall have —if we have the good sense to take steps to establish reciprocal relations which will in addition give Cuba herself a chance to live and carry out the obligations we have put upon her —in all probability, in from five to eight years, $150,000,000 to $200,000,000 per year of trade.

The powers of the Military Governor were absolute in every particular, and yet there was but one instance of a reversal of the action of the native court; this exception being for reasons which were published in full in the Official Gazette in Havana, and which met with general approval. The basis of the action taken by the Military Governor in this case has since been adopted as a basis to govern in similar cases. The courts have been untrammeled in the exercise of their authority, and the municipalities have been governed by officials elected by the people at the polls.

VII

THE government was transferred as a going concern. All the public offices were filled with competent, well trained employees; the island was free from debt and had a surplus of a million and a half dollars in the treasury; was possessed of a thoroughly trained and efficient personnel in all departments; completely equipped buildings for the transaction of public business; the administration of justice was free; habeas corpus had been put in force; police courts had been established; a new marriage law on lines proposed by the Roman Catholic Bishop of Havana, giving equal rights to all denominations, was in operation; the people were governed, in all municipalities, by officials of their own choice elected at the polls; trials in Cuban courts were as prompt as in any State of the Union, and life and property were absolutely safe; sanitary conditions were better than those existing in most parts of the United States; yellow fever had been eradicated from the island; modern systems of public education, including a university, high school and nearly three thousand seven hundred public schools, had been established; also well organized departments of charity and public works. The island was well supplied with hospitals and asylums, beggars were almost unknown. A new railway law had been promulgated; custom houses had been equipped and thoroughly established; the great question of church property had been settled; a basis of agreement between mortgaged creditors and debtors had been established; municipalities had been reduced from 138 to 82 in number; public order was excellent; the island possessed a highly organized and efficient rural guard; an enormous amount of public works had been undertaken and completed; harbors and channels were buoyed; old lighthouses had been thoroughly renovated and new ones built; in short, the government as transferred was in excellent running order. The great expense of organization and equipment was borne by the Military Government. At the time of the transfer, government buildings and equipment of every description were in such condition as to be able to render useful services for years at a small outlay compared to the cost incurred by the Military Government in renovating, building and purchasing the same. The insular government was undertaken without a dollar of public money on hand, except the daily collections of customs and internal revenue, and involved the collection and disbursement of $57,107,140.80, during its existence, for improvements in material conditions and the upbuilding of insular institutions. This sum does not include the municipal revenues, only the general insular revenues.

VIII

THE work called for and accomplished was the building up of a REPUBLIC, in a country where approximately 70 per cent. of the people were illiterate; where they had lived always as a military colony; where general elections, as we understand them, were unknown; in fact, it was a work which called for practically a rewriting of the administrative law of the land; including the law of charities and hospitals, public works, sanitary law, school law, railway law, etc.; meeting and controlling the worst possible sanitary conditions; putting the people to school; writing an electoral law and training the people in the use of it; establishing an entirely new system of accounting and auditing; the election and assembling of representatives of the people to draw up and adopt a constitution for the proposed new republic; in short, the establishment, in a little over three years, in a Latin military colony, in one of the most unhealthy countries of the world, of a republic modeled closely upon the lines of our own great Anglo-Saxon republic; and the transfer to the Cuban people of the republic so established, free from debt, healthy, orderly, well equipped, and with a good balance in the treasury. All of this work was accomplished without serious friction. The island of Cuba was transferred to its people as promised, and was started on its career in good condition and under the most favorable circumstances.

The government of Cuba while called "military" was so in name only. The courts exercised full and untrammeled jurisdiction from first to last. Means of appeal to the Supreme Court of Cuba from the decisions of the Military Governor were provided, in all cases except for appeals against such acts of the Military Government as were of a legislative character, such as the promulgation of laws, etc. Nearly all public offices were filled by

Cubans, and the government, as conducted, was as nearly a government by the people as was possible under conditions existing.

CAPITAL, LABOR AND THE GOLDEN RULE

I

WE have emerged successfully from the Great War. We are now confronted with the problems of peace, problems of readjustment which follow the war. They are many and their solution is vital to our progress and stability.

It is no time now for rash experiments or untried ideas. We must hold on to the policies and methods of established worth which experience has shown to be sound. We must progress, but we must know where we are going.

We must do all we can to encourage good business, whether it be big business or small business. If it is good business and beneficial to the public, it is worthy of encouragement; if it is bad business, we must control it and regulate it. Good business means prosperous labor, and this means increased production and nothing must be allowed to interfere with

19

ample production. It is the real remedy for
the high cost of living. Limitation on production is an invitation to disaster—disaster which
strikes first the poor but eventually affects all.
We cannot consider business and labor sepa-
rately. They are inter-locking and inter-de-
pendent. We must spread the war burden
over a much longer period of years than at
present contemplated. The present excess in-
come tax is paralyzing initiative. It is a
strangle hold upon the throat of business
which must be relaxed if American business is
to have that initiative which will be necessary
to give us our share in the world's trade. We
must do everything we can to help on good
business, for on it depends national prosperity.
Labor and Capital in this country must work
together in order to meet the problems which
are going to follow this world's war. We do
not wish an autocracy of either Capital or
Labor, but a real democracy in both, characterized by a spirit of co-operation and helpfulness. We must inject more of the human
element into our relations with those about us,
whether they be our associates or our subordinates—more gathering about the table and
discussing matters fully and frankly. We

must recognize that the workingman is neither
a machine nor a commodity, but that he is a
collaborator with capital. Individual capacity
and ambition must receive encouragement and
recognition. The employer must recognize
the dignity and status of the worker and give
him every consideration due. The closest possible contact and the fullest understanding
should be maintained between employer and
employee. Arrangements for the adjustment
of grievances must be provided which will
work smoothly and promptly. We must do
all we can to improve the worker's living conditions, to make his surroundings decent and
attractive to himself and family. His hours of
work must be such as to give him an opportunity for reasonable recreation with his
family during the hours of daylight. He
should receive a wage that not only permits
him to keep body and soul together, but en-
ables him to lay by something for the future.
If these conditions are to be obtained and
maintained, labor must recognize that high
wages can only be maintained under conditions
of high production and high efficiency. Capital must be paid in accordance with the risk of
the enterprise. Those who direct and plan

must be paid adequately, labor must be adequately paid, and after this, if anything remains, comes the question of an equitable distribution. Many of the more progressive, intelligent and far-seeing men are already beginning to give to labor a participation in this surplus—a share varying with its amount.

II

THE main thing is for Labor and Capital to pull together in the present great crisis, remembering that only through co-operation and frank and full understanding and mutual concessions can the wheels of industry be kept going.

You cannot legislate the Golden Rule into the hearts of men. Most of the difficulties between capital and labor are due to a failure to apply those basic principles. Theodore Roosevelt's great strength in this country was not due to the fact that he evolved so many new ideas. There are not many new ideas produced, there is not much that is new. But, he was constantly presenting to the American people old fundamental truths, sometimes in one garb and sometimes in another, but always in impressive array. There is nothing new in the Ten Commandments. There is nothing new in the Lord's Prayer. Yet, we say them over day after day, and year after year, and they lie at the very foundation of our religious and moral life; and they embody the basic principles for our personal conduct and our relations with other peoples. They are very simple and so are the basic principles which govern the relations between labor and capital. We must introduce into those relations more of the human element, more of that element of sympathy and association, more of the Golden Rule.

Labor is older than capital; capital comes from labor; nevertheless, they are one and inseparable. United they stand, separated they fall. If a man is going to handle labor successfully, it is not enough to give fair hours of work and fair wage—we must not only let live but help live.

III

WE must impress upon all, both labor and capital, the words of Abraham Lincoln, for they embody a sound doctrine which must govern: "Let not him who is houseless pull down the house of his neighbor; but, rather, let him strive diligently to build one for himself, thus, by example, showing confidence that his own when built shall stand."

We could not handle an army unless we had the human element and employed it very largely in dealing with our men. If we did not see the men every day, how they are housed, how they are fed, how they are clothed, how they are protected from the weather and looked after generally, they would soon lose interest in us and we would not have their loyal support. I think we have got to have a great deal more of that spirit with reference to labor. I think we must see how the women and children of those working for us are living. We must come more in contact with them. We cannot handle the matter in a purely academic way.

One of Theodore Roosevelt's greatest holds upon the American people was in his use of the human element; he always brought it into play. If he was in camp, no matter how rough and simple, he always had a good word to say about something. If the cook turned out a good breakfast he had a good word for him;

if he did not have a good breakfast he had a good word for him about something else. If the engineer of his train made a good run, he was never too busy to say, "Well, old man, you gave me a good run this morning and it was very important, too, that I be here." Just try a little of that with labor and see how it works.

IV

I HAVE had some labor groups to meet lately, and I have found about 95 per cent. of American labor is square and straight. Where they have had troubles, nine times out of ten it has been due to alien leadership of the type I have been urging that we get rid of in this country. Give them a square deal, put the thing up to them fairly, and you will be surprised to see how quickly they respond. Of course, you find men who do not respond to a square deal, but their numbers are small. I generally go on the assumption that every man in the organization intends to do his duty and I find that in about 98 per cent. of the cases I am right. You find obstinate and queer characters, you find many amusing incidents, but that is to be expected, and there is no use of becoming irritated. But if you assume that about 98 per cent. of all the people you have to deal with—be it in the army or in the navy or in your dealings with labor—are square, you will be surprised to find how true that assumption is.

I

THERE is a field into which the women
are coming and it is the big field. It is the field
of national politics. Personally, having seen
what the women did during the war, both at
home and abroad, I feel very confident that the
entrance of American women into the field of
American politics is going to have a very helpful and good effect. I think they are going to
bring a healthy influence. One which will
make our politics cleaner and introduce a better spirit into the political field.

I think women are going to do another
thing; I believe they are going to make the
men go to the polls, and if they do that they
will have done a good and helpful piece of
work. There is too much indifference among
people like ourselves. The danger within our
gates today is not so much the alien element,
although that is rather prominent at the mo-

ment, as it is our own indifference. We want all our people interested in their civic duties—both men and women. You cannot have a successful representative government unless all classes of people discharge their citizenship duties loyally and well.

You women have been dreaming for many years of bringing about certain results; you have dreamed of establishing better conditions of public and private morality; you have been thinking of and hoping to establish better housing conditions for the poor, of doing away with child labor; hoping to establish better conditions as to the training of children, and to bring about various regulations which will do away with vice and diseases which are a menace to our civilization. All those things are going to be possible for you if you come into the party organizations, whichever one you decide to join. Do not go into politics in little groups of women. Go in on a footing of absolute equality with men, and in equal or even greater numbers and play the game straight through, remembering that you can only accomplish results through organization.

II

WE have reason to be proud of the work of American women during the war. I do not know of any part of the country where American women did not take hold of the situation with keen energy. I know from personal experience in the Middle West and neighboring states the women did everything humanly possible to send our men overseas sound in body and clean in soul. They looked after the men in the towns near the camps; they maintained excellent conditions of public morality; they looked after the men when they were en route to the sea; they were at the ports of embarkation to give the last help they could give, and when the men arrived on the other side they found American women scattered at various points of activity from the ports of debarkation up to the fighting line. We found the women of the Red Cross, the women of the Salvation Army, and others, actually in the battle area doing their work. In fact, the work of women in all kinds of war activities was wonderful.

Some one wrote me and asked what I thought about the work of women in the war.

I answered very briefly and said that without the work of women during the war we could not have taken our part in it as we did. I do not think there was any class of our population more earnest than American women in carrying on the war to an effective and victorious end.

III

MANY States in the United States already have Woman Suffrage and women have been given a proper participation in municipal and political affairs. Many women have already been appointed to office. The work that they can do on the police force in dealing with women and the work which they can do as officers in many branches of municipal government is clearly evident to everybody. The part that women played in the Great War as nurses, canteen workers, and in selling Liberty Bonds, is also well known to all. The moral force that women will exert in performing their municipal and national duties will be very considerable. Indeed every woman did some kind of war work and their efficiency has been very well proved.

School affairs ought certainly to have the voice of the woman heard in them because she is so closely connected with the education of her children. The problems of child labor are also being very successfully attacked by women welfare workers. The conditions of vice are being diminished owing to their efforts. They will undoubtedly wield a greater influence on the affairs of the nation with the passing of time and as their efforts in the new field of suffrage become more evident.

IV

THE great bulk of women workers in the shops, in the mills and the factories, as well as the offices, and the training that they have received will stand them in good stead as their opportunities to gain suffrage approach. During any period of disturbance, strikes, war, revolution, the women suffer most. It was so in the beginning, it was so during all the days of history; and it is so today. The wailings of the women of captured cities have been echoed and re-echoed down the pages of history from time immemorable. The cries of the women of Russia today are being heard around the world.

The home is the cornerstone of our modern civilization. Woman is the center of the home. From the home emanate the teachings and morals and religion and the things we hold most dear. Anything that tends to destroy the home or diminish its influence is the greatest menace to the fundamentals of our civilization. All wars and revolutions threaten the security and the influence of the home and the protection of women. Consequently any movement that advocates any kind of violence or disorder should be combated by all the women of the land with all the weapons in their power.

WAR AND PEACE

I

THERE is nothing new in the movement
for peace. It is centuries old. Men have
dreamed of it since they had things of value
to hold. Women have prayed for it through
ages. Good people have looked forward to
the day of peace and tranquillity since the beginning of written history, and doubtless long
before. Just as they have desired to avoid
great misfortunes, plagues, earthquakes, fire,
or famine, so they have struggled to escape
war, except in those instances where war was
the lesser of two evils. Yet war is with us today, was with us yesterday, and so through all
the years since history records man's action or
tradition tells of his deeds.

Today, initiated as a rule with more formal-
ity, conducted with greater regard for the lives
of the noncombatants, and characterized by a
larger measure of observance of the dictates
of humanity in the treatment of prisoners and

the helpless, war is still with us. Peace leagues
struggle to prevent it; great alliances attempt
to abate it through preponderant forces—
through war itself, if need be.

II

ARBITRATION serves to lessen it a little
through disposing of many minor questions
which, if allowed to grow, might bring about
disputes resulting in war. As one of the
means of possible avoidance of a resort to
force, we welcome arbitration with open arms
and strive to give it the largest measure of
success, although realizing that in many cases
it will not avail to prevent that final resort to
force which can only be avoided when all great
Powers think alike. That time will come only
when absolutely unselfish justice marks international relations; when trade is equitably
shared among competing peoples; when competition, greed, selfishness, race interests and
prejudices and religious intolerance pass
away; when men and nations have no fixed
convictions which differ from those of others;
when they neither dream dreams nor see
visions. Until then, strive as we may, the cry

will be "Peace! Peace!" and yet there will be
no permanent peace. Nevertheless, we must
strive unceasingly to reduce war to the minimum, and to build up arbitration, but in so
doing we must not lose sight of the fact that
our efforts will not always be successful.

III

AN infinite wisdom has established the conditions under which we live and put in being
the great law which runs through the universe:
The law of the survival of the most fit. We
may struggle against it, but it rules in its general application. The most fit in a military
way, which includes good bodies, based on
good food, careful sanitation, well thought-
out training, clear intelligence resting on good
schools and early training, good armament,
equipment and organization, all springing
from intelligence and education applied to
self-protection and expansion of interests and
trade, will win in war just as they win in commerce.

They may not be the most fit in abstract
morality as relates to business relations between individuals or nations, or with regard to

generosity or sense of justice. The character-
istics of selfishness, self-interest and the spirit
of acquisitiveness are often accompanied by a
development of the means to get what is
coveted and to hold it securely. Human
nature in the mass is still human nature; under
a little more restraint, perhaps, but still the old
complex proposition of the ages, characterized
and controlled only too often by expediency
and self-interest.

IV

NATIONS are but collections of individuals; we need courts for the individual man,
and courts are of no avail without the police.
In the vast group of individuals constituting a
community, city or nation, the resort to force
by small groups representing perhaps a
thousandth, or less, of the population, is a
nuisance and is not permitted by the great
aggregation of the individuals among whom
they live, as it interferes with the interest and
activities, often safety, of too many other
people. The individuals in the community of
nations are few in number, and it is much less
easy to bring preponderant force to the control or restraint of the more powerful.

Yet as men struggle within the community
and too often resort to force unless restrained,
so do nations struggle and resort to force in
the world community, only here counter force
in the form of international police has never
been resorted to. Can it be effectively done
while there still exist strong groups characterized by century-old prejudices of race and interest? This is one of the great questions of
the hour. While considering it we should not
neglect preparation for defense or fail to
recognize conditions as they are.

v

THE maintenance of peace and the preven-
tion of war have been attempted through alliances to compel or regulate the action of
other groups or other combinations of nations,
by efforts so to group nations as to maintain
the balance of power between people whose
territorial expansion and increase of population and interests might otherwise jeopardize
peace. These efforts have usually resulted in
war sooner or later, although in many instances serving to maintain peace for long
periods. The policy of no combination satis-

fies the greed, ambition or policy of all its members, and eventually the dominating interest of one or more members of such a combination, or the injection of new interests or conditions, serves after a time to bring about the loosening of the bonds of the alliance and the formation of new combinations, too often with a resort to force as the final argument.

Thus far we see little prospect of change. We may hold down for a time the explosive pressure or give it a safe vent, but from time to time human effort will fail and the explosion will occur. In other words, the controlling nations are too few in number and their vital interests are so coincident or interwoven with those of the controlled nations that constant changes and rearrangements result in this grouping, and these changes inevitably bring about an appeal to force. It is difficult to see how this condition can be changed so long as national lines exist and racial groups continue, or certain trade areas remain under the control of these groups.

VI

JUSTICE and righteousness are not
enough to insure protection, nor is an upright
and blameless personal or national life a guarantee against the unscrupulous. A Pilate was
found to crucify Christ; and a strong, aggressive nation, believing in its own worth and
right to expand, has always been prone to
crush and coerce a weaker one, regardless of
the abstract justice of the weaker nation's
cause.

Why all these things are, is a question which
this world cannot answer in precise terms, and
with such answer we are not at this moment
concerned.

We can with justice say that public and
national morality is largely the reflection of
the education of our youth. Sound moral
training in the home, a healthy body and
a developed sense of justice and fair play,
probably make the sound, just and normal
man in public life, the best citizen, and, collectively, when assembled in legislative bodies or
engaged in executive or administrative work,
the man will act on the most just, reasonable
and tolerant lines. But even among men of

this class there will be strong differences of opinion and it is little short of folly to assume the contrary. We may diminish the frequency of strife and make more humane the struggle, but for the present nothing more.

VII

BLOOD, race, tradition, trade and a host of other influences, capped by ambition to go on, to lead, to expand, will always produce strife. We cannot escape this conclusion if we take as our guide the evidence of things done and being done, rather than follow the dictates of fancy or desire. The struggle for peace is centuries old, and efforts to end war and establish undisturbed peace have filled the minds of men and taxed the resources of nations. The great combinations of power to prevent war were, after all, the combinations of forces to restrain the exercise of force, and have more often than not ended in a great struggle for readjustment of the balance of power.

The theories and policies of addled minds and shallow intelligences, products of the applause of the lecture platform, or of minds

upset by the flattery incident to sudden wealth,
have had their share of attention, and even of
sympathy. After all, they indicate only a failure to understand that war generally has its
roots running deep below the surface that is
swept by the gaze of such observers. The
authors of these theories never have studied
seriously the causes of war. They assign as
causes the little incidents which serve to touch
off the mass of explosive which other forces
have been accumulating and piling up for a
generation or perhaps a century.

VIII

WAR, whether it be for evil or good, is
among men, and our clear duty is to recognize
this fact, instead of denying the evidence of
our senses simply because it is disagreeable
and brutal, something that we would get rid
of. Our duty is to protect ourselves as best we
can against war and build our protection on so
secure a foundation and maintain its efficiency
so systematically that our own institutions,
ideals and interests may be secure and that we
may be able to hand down to our children all
the benefits we have received from our fathers.
God has given us eyes to see, ears to hear, and

intelligence and memory to glean and carry from the lessons of the past something of wisdom to guide us in meeting the issues of the present. If we fail to make the best use of those faculties which have been given us, we must pay the penalty.

IX

WE must continue to strive for world peace, for the betterment of human conditions; we must do what we can to promote arbitration, love of justice; but we have no right to forget that none of these will serve to protect us against an unjust aggressor. Let us do all these good things, but at the same time take those measures of wise precaution which the experience of time and of all people teaches, that we may be prepared to defend with force those things which justice, honesty and fair dealings are inadequate of themselves to defend? As Cromwell said: "Trust in God— but keep your powder dry." In other words, do right, but do not trust to that alone. The highwayman is not especially concerned with the morals of the man whose purse he covets, nor is the great nation struggling for trade and expansion disposed to give especial consideration to the morals of the people standing in her way. Every nation does, however, give serious and prompt heed to the strength and ability of another to hold and protect what she has.

I

I BELIEVE we should adopt the League of Nations with reservations which thoroughly Americanize it and leave America absolutely untrammeled to follow the dictates of the American people, expressed through the agencies provided by the Constitution.

Whatever comes out of this discussion of the League of Nations, there is one thing we should try to preserve, and that is the machinery whereby the representatives of the different nations can get together around a table to talk things over before a resort to force. You do not fight with any less determination if you give the other fellow a chance to talk, and we do need something through which we can get together and talk things over.

In urging the building up of a strong national spirit, I do not mean that we are to be lacking in international charity or in the spirit of international helpfulness, but if we have a strong and vigorous national spirit, we shall be a real power for good. We want a spirit which will stand for international fair dealing and a willingness to help in world crises, such as that through which we are now going. In other words, "we want to speak softly, but carry a big stick," that is to say, be just and fair but also be strong and ready to support the right, not only with words but with force if necessary.

II

IF WE are to be a great force for maintaining the peace of the world, a great influence for good, we must have not only honesty and integrity of purpose, but we must have organized and at our hands the forces of right. We can be strong without becoming aggressors. We can have weapons without turning them against our brothers. We can organize against the forces of wrong doing without becoming an enemy of the right. It is not enough to mean well, to desire that the right shall prevail, but we must have the organization and preparedness to serve our ideals.

III

I BELIEVE that we should accept the
League of Nations as modified and safeguarded by the existing Lodge reservations—
reservations that Americanize it and safeguard
our traditional policies, reservations which
leave America absolutely free and untrammeled to follow the will of her own people in
all questions of foreign and domestic policy.

I, of course, at all times favor getting the
views of the people of the country where it is
practicable. However, in view of the fact that
the people have clearly indicated—as I see it
—that they are in favor of the treaty if our
traditional policies, interests and freedom of
action are fully safeguarded, it seems unnecessary to delay this most important question for
a general election in which their views could
hardly be more decisively expressed than they
have already been.

IV

WITH reference to my views on our foreign policy, I am in favor of and shall continue
to be in favor of the well-established policy of

this Government which conserves and promotes the interests of our own country. I do not think this treaty with the reservations impairs that policy. It does not entangle us; it leaves us free to exercise our own judgment; it is temporary. If we choose to have it so, we can retire on two years' notice.

One aim of America's foreign policy has always been the promotion of the peace of the world. In order to accomplish this end her people must be free in any given situation to stand for righteousness according to their judgment. As an important means to that end, instrumentalities should be created and developed by which, consistently with this freedom, the momentum of the other free and peace-loving nations of the world, acting concurrently with us, can be added to our efforts.

THE FARMER—HIS RIGHTS AND WRONGS

I

AGRICULTURE is the principal source of our wealth. The farmers are the stable, conservative element. They stand for good government, for the rights of property and the rights of men. The Red Flag never flies over a farmhouse.

The decrease in agricultural production compared with the increase in the population of the country and the number of people who live and work on the farms is disastrous and should not continue. In other words, the food supply should never be allowed to fall below the country's requirements. We ought always to be self-sustaining.

During the war, under every sort of handicap, the farmers of America rendered magnificent service in producing the food necessary to feed not only the United States but very largely our Allies. They sent their sons to

war and in spite of the shortage of labor and
by dint of increased effort they tremendously
increased this country's output of food. Had
they not done so, it would have been impossible for us to have taken our part in the war
as we did. The war would have dragged on
and probably been lost. Now the farmers feel
that their service was not adequately recognized.

The farmers constitute a full third of our
population, and the welfare of the nation is
practically bound up with theirs. Yet the
benefits of modern civilization have not been
extended to our rural communities in any such
measure as they have a right to demand.

Education for farm children should be uni-
versally accessible. Rural schools should be
up to the standards of city schools in every
way. The little state of Denmark, we are told,
has managed to build up a system of rural
schools that leads the world. No doubt this
explains the reason why Denmark leads the
world in agricultural productivity per acre
under cultivation. There is no reason why we,
with our greater resources, cannot duplicate
Denmark's feat, even outstrip it. Moreover,
if we are to keep up our national progress, we

must see to it that our farming population has comparatively equal educational, social, political and economic advantages with our urban population.

II

LONG hours of labor, lack of proper returns, and lack of social and intellectual attractions are largely responsible for the constant flow of young men and women from the farms to the towns and cities. We have done little or nothing to make farm surroundings more attractive or farm labor less of a drudgery. We have not developed our rural highways and modes of communication as they should be.

Every sound and normal man and woman should have a fair and workable chance to earn a living and to receive the benefits of their toil, a fair and workable chance for a decent, useful and desirable life, with a chance to marry and support a family, and give the children a reasonable opportunity for a reasonable start.

The farmers have a right to expect from every national administration a Department of Agriculture in full and intelligent co-operation with them and the great farm organizations of America. They deserve to be given the results of thorough and intelligent study as to the cost of farm products at home and abroad, and should be furnished the uncensored facts.

We must keep constantly in mind one most important fact, which is that nothing must be permitted to interfere with ample production. There must be no fixing of prices which will result to the detriment of the farmer. Indeed, price fixing, especially minimum price fixing, should be entered into most cautiously and only when it is certain that good and not harm will result.

I believe in a far larger measure of direct dealing between producers and consumers of food. Today altogether too small a portion of the consumer's dollar gets back to the farmer. In Omaha the other day I met a farmer who was getting his breakfast at a hotel in the city. He said to me: "I sell my milk at six o'clock in the morning at eight cents and three hours later I find it selling at fifteen cents. After a year's work—for I raised the cow, fed her, milked her and brought the milk to market—I get only eight cents.

After three hours' work another fellow gets fifteen cents. Some one in between gets seven cents in a few hours. How does he do it? That's what I want to find out." The farmer feels that he has a right to sell directly to the consumer wherever he can. Means should be furnished him for greatly amplifying his opportunity in this direction.

III

I BELIEVE, and I think most persons who have given the matter thought will agree with me, that we have permitted too much of speculation to grow up in the handling of life necessities. I think there can be no question that the number of middlemen in trade can be reduced with advantage to our economic life, to both producer and consumer. While the storage of food supplies is absolutely necessary to feed our people, since crops are not produced throughout the year, the hoarding of food supplies should be severely punished and vigorously suppressed.

Much has been done in the way of co-operation among the farmers of Europe; co-operation in marketing their products and co-operation in purchasing. Big business and large or-

ganizations of workingmen have come to realize that the best results are often obtained by
co-operation. This should not involve dis-
crimination against any man who chooses to
work for himself, because there are always
positions in which individual work is the best.

I believe that co-operative organizations of
farmers should be given the same consideration as to other organizations under similar
circumstances.

Secure provision should be made to enable
farmers to obtain adequate credit so as to de-
velop and improve their land. Steps should
be taken to increase the production of necessary fertilizers, so that the farmer may never
be without an adequate supply. Steps should
be taken looking to the increased production
of nitrates. We are still dependent for our
nitrates upon importations from Chile, and in
case of war with a power controlling the seas
this great supply of fertilizers would be cut
off. We should push forward at once the completion of the nitrate producing plants com-
menced during the war. It is very essential
that the country should be entirely self-sup-
porting and in no way dependent upon other
nations for fertilizers.

IV

THE gradual abolition of farm tenancy would be a healthy development. Since our earliest beginnings, the typical farmer has owned the land and has cultivated it with the aid of his own sons and a few hired men. We do not wish this type of farmer to be supplanted by one who holds his lands as a tenant. We do not wish to see the farmers absorbed by the big land holders to the detriment of our best farming interests. The tenant farmer should be encouraged through a liberal system of credits to buy and own his land. Tenant farming generally means the exhaustion of the soil. The tenant farmer takes out as much as possible from the soil and puts in as little as he can. The result is the gradual falling off of production from one of the most serious of all causes, deterioration of the soil.

We want to maintain the traditional type of farmer—the man who lives upon and owns the land. To do this we must make his life and surroundings as attractive and comfortable as possible. The man who owns the land and tills it is the man who stands for good government, conservation, the rights of property, law and order—in fact, for those basic principles which give a nation stability and life.

A wide extension of the present Farm Bureau System, in co-operation with various State agricultural departments and local committees, seems to me most desirable. It ought to solve many of the economic questions which confront the farmer, problems which are ever-varying, problems of production and distribution. All this work should be done under the expert advice, guidance and assistance of the Government.

One of the great problems which confront us is not only to keep up an agricultural population, but to increase it. By multiplying the farmer's opportunities for improving his farm and production we will continue to make this a self-sustaining nation. The moment the output of farms falls below the demands of our people, new and grave problems will confront us.

In order to keep up increasing interest in agriculture we must give heed to existing conditions of discontent and take intelligent steps to remedy them. The increase in urban population at the expense of rural and agricultural means increased unrest, increased cost of living and diminished stability. Let us give to the agricultural class the attention it deserves.

v

IN building up the republic of Cuba from the wreck of a war-worn Spanish colony, I turned my attention first to order and to agriculture as the foundations upon which the structure must rest. The returns were marvelous. We pushed forward agriculture as rapidly as possible. Taxation was suspended on all estates whose owners were attempting to put them under production. Farmers were furnished food, supplies and implements which enabled them to live on the farm and plant and harvest their crops. Animals were imported an l turned over to farmers on easy terms, securities being taken in form of liens on property. Import duties on all agricultural and plantation supplies and machinery were reduced to merely nominal rates. The result was that in a very short time agriculture was in a most flourishing condition, and, figuratively speaking, for every dime of outlay there was a dollar in return. The sugar crop jumped from 200,000 tons per year to nearly 1,200,000 tons in less than three years, and tobacco increased in proportion. The money received from crops was expended largely in rehabilitating the island. Revenues increased; peace and tranquillity went hand in hand with advancing agriculture. Today the foundation of the prosperity of the island of Cuba rests squarely on its agriculture.

VI

THERE should be much more attention paid to the development of stock throughout the country. I shall never forget the words of the Secretary of Agriculture of the Argentine Republic when I commented on the tremendous prices the Argentine was paying for selected stock for breeding purposes: "Oh, yes, we do pay high prices; but for every dollar we pay for good stock we get back hundreds of dollars from increased quality." And as one looked at the great beef herds of square, blocky Herefords, one could understand what he meant. So it was with all other lines of stock whether cattle, horses or sheep. To secure the best of stock was the object of the government. There is no question that much more could be done advantageously by our Government to aid in the improvement of stock without any great increase in expense to the farmer.

I

THERE is much work to be done in behalf of our public schools. The draft showed a very alarming condition of physical unfitness. Practically fifty per cent of the American men between the ages of twenty-one and thirty-one were unfit for hard front-line service. That is a rather alarming condition. It is bad enough from a military standpoint; it is infinitely worse from the standpoint of industry, and it is peculiarly sad when one remembers that most of the defects, at least a very large percentage of them, could have been done away with by a thorough calisthenic training in the public schools. I think that is one thing we ought to interest ourselves in, to strive to better the training in the public schools.

We need a broader moral training in public schools. I do not mean narrow sectarian training, but we must teach more of the broad moral principles. We want to teach in our schools at all times a spirit of truth, of fair play, the square deal, honesty and loyalty, devotion, good citizenship, and the spirit of service and sacrifice. All these ought to be built up in the schoolroom, and in that connection very serious consideration ought to be given to the condition of your teaching forces in both universities and public schools.

II

TEACHERS are very much underpaid. There is no class today in America which has the opportunity to do more important or more constructive work in the building up of good citizenship, I do not know that I could except the church itself, than those who are teaching in our universities and schools. They are forming the men and women of tomorrow. They are working quietly but effectively day after day, week after week and month after month. They have our children with them much more than we have them, and as they incline the minds of these youngsters so will they be later on. They are not only implanting knowledge, evoking power and teaching the children how to use the knowledge they give them, but they are also waging that silent battle against ignorance and prejudice upon the successful outcome of which depends very largely the stability of this country. The average country school teacher in many sections of this country receives less than the average first-class chauffeur. The college professor is not paid as well as the average good bricklayer, and the result has been that since the war many of our ablest professors and teachers have had to seek employment in other lines of work.

III

WE want in this country for our teaching force men and women of the very best intelligence, and of the highest character. Many of the very best are staying, it is true, because they have the missionary spirit, because of love of the work. The teaching force of America is making the citizens of tomorrow, and it is a most important duty. Pay them well and treat them well.

We talk of other things, and of many progressive ideas, and so forth, but one of the big, practical things is to see to it that the teaching force of America is given the recognition which it is entitled to, because you cannot trifle with the education and training of your children. As your children are trained and educated, so will the Ship of State be tomorrow.

The security of our Republic rests largely on the educational system of the States.

We want to put into our high schools a great deal more of sound, economic training than we have hitherto. We ought to give at least the fundamentals of economic training in the lower schools, and in the high schools it ought to be gone into pretty thoroughly. That an honest day's wage means an honest day's work; that the real remedy for the high cost of living is increased production; that the real enemies of labor are those who talk reduced production. We want to drive some of those ideas home. When our children go out from the schools and colleges they want to have more than a mere superficial knowledge of many things; so let us teach a little more of these basic, homely principles, and let us try to drive home, too, something more in the way of information as to what our Government stands for, how it is run, how it is operated, what the Constitution means, what is meant by the Constitutional guarantee.

We want to impress upon all our children that the Constitution is vital to our national life, and that every step we have taken away from it has been a step toward chaos.

Immigration Without Assimilation

I

WE must give more care to our immigration. We must look into the quality of our immigration. We have put all the sand into our cement that it will stand. There is no use having the portals open on the one hand for the deportation of the alien Red and wide open on the other hand for the admission of the undesirable immigrant.

We need a certain amount of immigration, but we have a right to know something of the quality of the people who come here, and we are negligent in our duty if we do not ascertain very carefully what the quality of those people is. It is not enough that they shall be physically sound and of reasonable mental intelligence, but we have a right to know whether they come from the anarchistic group, whose religion is destruction and whose object is the ruin of all government. We do not want this class to come into this country.

As we look over Europe today we see this great wave of unrest, the so-called Red movement. It is beating now on the frontiers of Hungary, it is beating against the remnants of the German army; you find North Italy under martial law, and in Spain you find great unrest. You find France bled white by war, trying to re-establish order and prosperity, to rebuild a devastated country and start again the wheels of commerce. In England you have another nation bled white by war but struggling tremendously and with great intelligence and energy to re-establish her commerce and gain the main trade areas.

We do not know just why this unrest has come to our country, but to a certain extent it has come. We do not want to have this element increased. We should deport the man who comes here determined to tear down our institutions, and we should deport him through due legal processes, but very promptly. There is no use of arresting thousands of people in a spectacular manner and then failing to deport them if they are found unfit to be citizens.

II

I THINK we ought to look over the people who are coming here, just as we look over men and women before we give them a passport in time of war. They go to our consular and diplomatic agents and are examined very carefully before a passport is issued. We ought to have a searching examination of the immigrants who are coming to America now and in the future.

You know these people are going to live among you; their children are going to marry your children; their blood is going to be intermingled with yours. We are all of us interested in the maintenance of the highest possible standard in America, and we must look much more carefully to immigration into our country than we have in the past.

When these people arrive I think we ought to hold them for a time under observation; not for a long time, but long enough to give them a course in intensive Americanization and teach them what our Government stands for, the difference between liberty and license, and impress upon them that here true liberty is found within the law and never outside of it;

try to give them an idea of the conditions under which they are going to live.

What happens now? As soon as the immigrant comes ashore he goes to live usually in a racial area, to be fed on a dialect press. I think we ought to try to obviate that and to use our best influence to have these people go to sections of the country where their previous training will be of the most use to us, and of the greatest value to them; where they will have the best opportunity to succeed. New York, for instance, is the largest Italian city in the world, and some of our other cities have enormous racial groups, and there they are in congested racial masses, fed by a dialect press and retaining the ideals and prejudices of their own lands, at times even stronger than they were in the old country.

III

WE are glad to welcome the immigrant who comes here to adopt our institutions and live up to our standards and ideals. If he comes with the intention of becoming a part of us and to support our Government, we are glad to have him; but we should turn our faces like flint against the class of people who are coming here with avowed dislike for our institutions and with declared intention of pulling down our Government. We ought not, with this condition of unrest prevailing throughout the world, receive this kind of people. We have the right and the moral obligation to our own people of today and those who will live tomorrow, to see that the people who are coming here to be the Americans of tomorrow are of the right kind; that they are for us and not against us.

While we are proud that America is called the home for the oppressed, let us see to it that she does not become the dumping ground of the degenerate.

IV

AMERICANIZATION of the alien and some native born is one of the great tasks before us. We have got to drive this home to our people. Our work is not going to be limited entirely to foreigners and those who have come to us and have not been assimilated, but it has to be applied to a good many who have been born here. We want to get rid of the

Red element, ship it out, keep any more from coming in, and take hold of the problem of Americanization very seriously among our newcomers. Teach them to love our flag. They may have a sentimental fondness for their own flag and own language. We want to stand, however, in this country for one language in the public schools, for one flag and one loyalty, and we must do it if we are going to build up that spirit of solidarity which we want. We want to build up an intense American spirit; not a selfish spirit but an intense American spirit, America, first and a long way first. This is what we want. And, we should have behind that spirit an American conscience, a conscience which will make this nation do its duty whenever called upon to do it, and do it promptly.

In these days there is a good deal of talk of mandates, but the mandate that our people will always accept is that mandate which comes from the conscience of the American people. That is the mandate which Americans will respond to and no other.

We have one such mandate now. It is that we, with the wealth that has come to us, shall do all that is humanly possible to alleviate the conditions of destitution and suffering in Europe. This does not mean sending men overseas arms in hand; nor does it involve us in the intrigues of European diplomacy, but it means simply doing our duty as a Christian nation. There are literally millions of people who stand without shelter, without food, without necessary clothing. It is a condition unparalleled in the world's history. It is a condition we can do a lot to alleviate and in doing it we make no enemies, we become entangled in no entangling alliances.

I

WE need a highly efficient but small Regular Army, 200,000 to 250,000 men, sufficient for the peace needs of the nation, and a first-class Navy, always ready.

We must have a definite and well-established policy of national preparedness. Never again must we permit America to be caught so utterly unprepared and unready as we were in the Great World War. We paid for this lack of preparation in blood and treasure. We grant universal suffrage; we must demand universal obligation for service in peace and war whenever the nation calls. To fail to do this is to deny the basic principles upon which the Republic rests, equality of opportunity and equality of obligation within the limit of our powers.

The Army of the Republic should be built up with the idea of maintaining the smallest number of men living the lives of professional soldiers, only enough to give us an army sufficient for the peace needs of the nation, but behind it some system which will give our youth enough training to make them quickly available in case of attack.

II

WE must insure the largest possible amount of security, together with the absolute avoidance of anything un-American or militaristic.

We won't call it compulsory military training, but training for national service which will combine vocational, industrial and citizenship training. They all go together in the making of the American citizen.

We are concerned with the making of better, more effective men. The soldier training is only a part in the making of the citizens of the Republic.

The young men who have been through this war are the men to whom this country is going to look for a military policy. It has got to be an American military policy on purely democratic lines, but there must be some kind of policy, and when we get over the war weariness and give our attention to home affairs the country is going to look to the American Legion to outline a military policy, one founded on the wisdom of experience.

We should have a strong but conservative foreign policy, not an aggressive or bullying policy, but the foreign policy indicated in the words of Theodore Roosevelt, "Speak softly but carry a big stick." He believed in a foreign policy which assured the safety of American citizens who are living within the laws of the land of their abode, no matter where. You remember when an American was captured by some North African bandit the words of Roosevelt, "Perdicaris alive or Raisuli dead." That has the American ring and means safety to Americans and American interests.

AMERICANIZATION

I

IF Theodore Roosevelt were here now, I believe that he would feel the same keen interest that we do in the great issues of the day. The war is over, but the problems after the war are confronting us and they are rather large and some of them are rather serious. We want to bring to the solution of these problems the same kind of enthusiasm, the same coöperation of effort, that we have brought to the conduct of the war. We want to do all we can first toward Americanizing the newcomers. We have been doing our work very superficially thus far. Marching in the street parades and carrying banners, while the national air is being played, is not Americanization.

We want to take up very systematically and earnestly real Americanization. I think we want to have throughout the graded public

schools but one language. I think the slogan
ought to be that in the graded schools of this
country there should be only one language
and that language the language of the Declaration of Independence.

II

WE want to build up a strong, intense
American spirit, not selfish, but a real American spirit. We must avoid dangerous internationalism as we would avoid death, for it
means national death. There must be a strong,
well-balanced nation. We want an intense
national spirit, helpful to the world in trouble,
but still American, and we want behind it an
American conscience which will make America
always quickly responsive to her duties. We
want a real American conscience, a Christian
conscience.

Americanization is a vital subject in these
days when there is so much unrest in the world.
The Red menace is rapidly sweeping over
Europe. We are looking on the rather thin
line of the defenders of the integrity of Hungary and Poland, and we wonder whether that
thin line is going to be strong enough to hold

up the force of disorganization. We find the spirit of unrest in Spain and all over Europe. We find it here. But I think that the manifestations of unrest are only psychological phases. They are here because they are in Europe.

We are going to govern this country by Americans. When I say Americans I do not mean necessarily people whose families have been here many generations. But I mean the real Americans, the people who have adopted and are trying to live up to our standards and ideals, the people who stand for law and order, who stand for government under the Constitution, who adhere to a policy that has made us what we are, who are ready to offer everything, even life itself, for this country. These are the men and women who are going to govern this country.

III

WE want to make it possible for the good foreigners, who wish to come to our country and become American citizens and live by our form of government, to come to our land; but we do not want to be a dumping ground for radicals, agitators, Reds, who do not understand our ideals, who do not know what our ancestors suffered to build up our institutions and who have no respect for our flag. This can be done by a more careful scrutiny of the immigrants who apply for admission to our country. If we do this, it will save us a great deal of the agitation which has been frequent in this country for some time. We should also have an organized system for distributing the desirable foreigners in sections of the country where they can do the things that they have learned to do. Those who have been farmers ought to go to the country. Those who have been skilled tradesmen, to the trades and to the factories of the kind that they have been trained in. In this way we shall be able to absorb the foreigners more readily than if they go into the highly congested neighborhoods where only people of their own nationalities live.

IV

THE I. W. W. is like a plague of infected rats. At Omaha, they drugged the crowd with booze. The Reds are a menace to the country. The red flag is a menace to our country.

We must strive to educate these foreigners in the ideals of Americanism. We must assure them that equality of opportunity is given to all to make the best of themselves; that all reforms in this country must be brought about in an orderly manner and that we believe in Americanism and not internationalism!

In this work of Americanizing, the employer can aid a great deal by insisting that the English language be spoken in the factories, the mills and the shops; in encouraging foreign laborers to attend night schools and to utilize the newspapers and other American journals so that they will familiarize themselves with current American public opinion, which is, after all, a great formative influence in our American political life. In short, if the employer will treat these foreigners, who are working for him, with as much consideration as he does his customers, a sympathetic bond could be established between these foreigners and their employers that could not very well be severed. It is the duty of every loyal American to do all in his power to help the country in the great task of absorbing the foreigner and Americanizing those who have come to our shores from foreign lands. If we all co-

operate in this work it will only be a question
of a short time before the doctrines of the Reds
will find no fertile fields to grow in, and we
shall hear no more about revolution and violence.

v

WE want to keep our feet on the ground
and hold on to the ideals and policies which
have made us great, to the Constitution and
the national policies whose wisdom has been
demonstrated by our security and progress.
We must do all we can to build up a sound
national spirit, an intense spirit of Americanism.

We must do all we can to complete the work
of infusing into one homogeneous mass of
Americans the various elements which make
up our population. We have had in our armies representatives of all the fighting groups
in Europe, and I want to say a word of appreciation of the loyalty of these new citizens,
of these Americans of alien descent. We were
a bit uncertain as to what some of them would
do, for some of them came from the blood
strains of our enemies, but we have only to
read the lists of our dead to realize that Ameri-

cans of German and other descent have been loyal. They have written anew their oath of allegiance. This time it has been written in their own blood.

These new people are now a part of us in every sense. They have offered their lives in defense of the country. They have stood prepared to make the supreme sacrifice and many have made it. So let us hear no more of hyphenated Americans, and look upon all who have been loyal and lived up to our ideals as Americans, for through their service and their loyalty they have measured up to the standard of true Americans.

I

MOST men, and practically all soldiers, believe in the principle of arbitration. They are anxious to see its application extended and amplified. Yet we must not be blind to the fact that it is not of general application. Arbitration can be resorted to only when both parties believe that there is something to be arbitrated. When one party to the controversy is confident it is right, is absolutely resolved to maintain the right and justice of its claims, arbitration appears neither desirable nor reasonable. Again, many questions are of vital importance to one nation and of little or no importance to another. The vitally interested party does not care to arbitrate these questions. For instance, we do not care to arbitrate questions of immigration. Nations have always guarded very jealously questions affecting citizenship, and have held that they are questions to be decided by the nation itself.

The Monroe Doctrine is another instance. This policy, of vital importance to us, is not generally approved by other nations. If we should submit to arbitration questions arising under it we should have difficulty in finding an impartial board. In the maintenance of the Monroe Doctrine we have had the unexpressed, but nevertheless strong, approval of England. So, too, the most vital questions leading to the present Great War have never been subjects of arbitration.

II

THERE are relatively few people who appreciate the true causes of war; who realize that the great majority of wars arise through differences or controversies concerning commerce, trade routes, trade areas, and lines of commercial expansion. Race expansion and, to a lesser extent than heretofore, religious differences are also causes of war. The great underlying causes, in most cases, run back directly to trade or to the possession of certain favorable areas for racial or industrial expansion. The old days when the arbitrary decision of kings ordinarily determined whether war was to be waged or peace maintained have practically passed away, and no leader or ruler in the present age would venture to involve his people in war unless he felt that he had their support.

III

THE plan for an alliance of nations to enforce world peace is not a new one. The desire for such peace has led to many earnest efforts to build up agreements and alliances which would insure it. Thus far such efforts have been without lasting success. Coincident with these efforts are declarations of men who, deeply impressed with the horrors of war, honestly believe that each great war is the last, and announce their conclusions to the world as statements of fact. Many men doubtlessly honestly believed before the beginning of the present great war that international strife on a large scale was passing away. Charlatans and tricksters and professional "peace-at-any-price" men backed up their arguments with the statement that war was at an end, hence there was no need of preparation. There is nothing new in this propaganda. It is as old as written history. War has been always one of those rugged paths of suffering through which nations have from time to time had to pass in the discharge of their duty toward themselves and in the upholding of principles of international morality and right. I do not now refer to wars of conquest. I am speaking simply of defensive wars or wars for great principles. Charles Sumner believed and stated in 1848 that the world had seen its last great war. Some of our professional pacifists of lighter timber and louder voices were proclaiming over the entire country up to the outbreak of the present war that the Balkan war was the last of the world's great wars. Block, the author of that remakable book, "The Future of War," which had much to do with the creation of the Hague Conference, gave extensive reasons why a great war could not again occur. Even our distinguished pacifists have predicted that war has passed out of the realm of possibility. All these statements are idle and wholly unwarranted, either from the standpoint of history or that of present conditions, or from that of the probabilities of the future, which must be judged very largely by the past.

IV

IN recent times we have had various alliances which are really alliances for the maintenance of peace. The Triple Alliance, the Triple Entente, the Entente Cordiale, are all marked efforts in this direction, all of which, as the recent Great War indicates, have been doomed to failure. I doubt very much whether this country will ever go into a world alliance and pledge herself to use her forces to maintain peace perhaps at the expense of a cause with which we may be in sympathy and more autocratic forms of governments not. Our best policy is to be ready to defend with our own arms and our own resources our territories, our rights, and our institutions. One of the dangers of the present effort in the line of an alliance to preserve peace by force of arms is that it still further delays the undertaking of absolutely necessary organization and preparedness.

The problem which confronts us is one of preparation, such preparation as will make all possible antagonists hesitate before forcing us to resort to war. An upright and just life does not protect the individual or the nation

against aggression. The best men who have
ever lived on this earth have suffered martyr-
dom, and inoffensive nations have been swept
ruthlessly aside by more powerful ones in
whose way they stood. All this is very un-
fortunate, but it is fact. Wars will become
less frequent when people are less selfish and
more moral. Universal responsibility for service will help build up, as much as anything
can, a habit of seriously considering and weigh-
ing the causes which may lead to war. It will
not prevent war. Wars will never cease until
human nature is radically changed. No nation can fold its hands and submit to oppres-
sion, be neutral in all things, both good and
bad, refuse to contest any issue, and continue
to exist. It will be swept aside and absorbed
by other and more vigorous peoples, or linger
an inert mass, subject to the will of others.

THE application of the principle of universal service brought to the colors through the draft, first and last, approximately three million men—men from all sections of the country and from all the races and race mixtures which make up our population.

It furnished an excellent opportunity to see the men of America as they are, and while the showing was splendid in all that which related to willingness to serve the Nation in time of war, either in the ranks or wherever sent, and to do their part in the great struggle for civilization and humanity, for good faith and fair dealing among nations, it brought to our attention certain conditions which are not only regrettable but alarming. Only about half of the men of military age are really fit for hard military service. This rating is based upon standards of physical excellence well below those of the Regular Army, Navy and Marine Corps in time of peace. The draft boards sent forward to the training camps 65 per cent of all who presented themselves for enrollment and were suitably examined by the board. Of those sent to the training camps an average of 7 per cent were rejected as unfit for any service, and a large percentage was sent to development battalions, and others to labor battalions, camp utilities, and special lines of work not requiring the best physical condition, so that, deducting all, it is safe to say that not over 50 per cent, probably less, of the men were fit for line service when the Nation was called to the colors.

II

IN some of the racial groups from certain sections vice diseases, active and latent but dangerous, were found amounting to over 30 per cent. Through all the draft there was a lamentable and alarmingly heavy percentage. The percentage was lower among men coming from the agricultural and ranching districts of the Middle-West and Northwest; much heavier among the colored than among the white race. The heaviest percentages, taking the men as a whole, were found among those coming from the large towns and manufacturing centers.

When it is remembered that the men sent to camps for training had passed selective draft boards, and that they represented those who were considered most fit to undergo training and preparation for military service, it does not take much imagination to picture the physical and health conditions of the remaining 29 per cent. Think what this condition means: what its effect is upon the race, upon national efficiency and national morality and character.

I believe that, generally speaking, the percentage of vice diseases was found to be lower in the sections of the country where women have taken an active part in public affairs, and in those sections of our country in which alcoholic liquors are not to be obtained. But throughout the nation the percentage is distressingly heavy, and indicates very clearly the need of stricter enforcement of the laws against vice and increasing efforts everywhere to stamp out the social evil.

III

THERE were numbers of men with digestive disturbances, great numbers with defective teeth, defective vision, minor curvatures and

deformities, flat feet, ruptures, either actual
or incipient; general defects in the way of flat
chests, stooping postures, ear troubles, and
large numbers of men suffering from hookworm, with its accompanying anæmia and
sluggishness of mind and muscle. Many of
these defects, in fact most of them, were in a
way unknown to the men. They had grown
up that way. They felt no special conscious-
ness of being physically defective. There were
many men in whom the co-ordination of mind
and muscle was very poor. Their impulses
were slow and their reaction sluggish. In
other words, the co-ordination of mind and
muscle was far from what it should have been.

While many of these defects were suscep-
tible of cure or of such improvement as would
render the men fit for some kind of service,
and to carry on the ordinary duties and labors
of men in time of peace, remember, always,
that these were among the 70 per cent who
represented those considered fit for service.
In the other 30 per cent much worse conditions existed. This is not an attractive picture; but it is one well worth considering and
studying with a view to the correction and betterment of conditions referred to.

IV

WHEN the men came to camp they were
thoroughly gone over, and those who were not
considered fit for full training were placed in
development battalions, where each man received such special treatment as his case de-
manded, and a large number of them were
eventually made fit for service. The men suffering from vice diseases were given the benefit
of the best possible treatment, and they were
held largely segregated until they were considered clean and safe to go among their fel-
low-men. Their curative treatment was carried on systematically even after their assign-
ment to organizations. When they were dis-
charged from the service it can be safely said
of the men with vice diseases that many of
them were sent back no longer active menaces
to society or unfit to become the fathers of a
race.

Taking the defectives as a class, as they came
out of the development battalions, the change
in appearance was remarkable. They were
entirely different-appearing men. They had
found themselves, or were at least well on the
way to so doing. Mind and muscle were bet-

ter co-ordinated. There had been a great improvement in all-around physical efficiency, and a marked increase in mental alertness and power of concentration. Of course, there were a considerable number who never became fit for military service, but almost without exception all had greatly improved.

Generally speaking, a serious effort was made to hold men who were dangerous to society until they were no longer so.

The mobilization of the selected men of our Nation brought to our attention an intolerable, unnecessary, and a dangerous condition, dangerous to us and to the race.

v

ONCE we have established throughout the land proper physical training in our schools, both public and private, the training which will give the youth of the country erect figures, a proper carriage, proper co-ordination of mind and muscle, the work in the training camp will be much easier and the percentage of men fit to serve their country much greater. When they come to the training camp for their military training, combined, as I hope it will be, with some form of industrial and vocational training, they will receive the final systematic setting up and corrective work, which will send them back to their communities better men physically, and, consequently, of greater economic value, better men from the citizenship standpoint and better men to be the fathers of a nation—men who will know that their sins will be visited upon their children's children, men with a better appreciation of the clean, decent and moral life.

Universal training for national service is worth all it may cost because of the physical betterment which will come through it, because it means a better all-around race of men and consequently a better people, a nation with a sound mind in a sound body.

Organized Good Samaritans

I

AMONG the most remarkable and useful developments of the war has been the growth and broadening of the field of effort of the American Red Cross and other organizations, some of them expressly organized to meet war conditions and all of them directed with a view to sending our troops overseas clean and sound in mind and body, and to helping in the conduct of the war.

Generally speaking, their work has been exceedingly well done—done with an effectiveness which is best appreciated by those who have been in contact with the troops in the great training camps, ports of embarkation and debarkation, and at the large railway distributing centers.

These organizations, individually and collectively, have been a great force for building up morale, and, hence, for winning the war.

The activities of these organizations have been extended, especially those of the Red Cross. Its efforts have not been limited merely to providing nurses, equipment of hospitals, preparation of surgical dressings, provision of supplies and aid for the sick and wounded. This organization has gone into the training camps, established itself at railway stations, at hospitals, military posts, and other points. It has distributed food, clothing, surgical equipment, supplies of various kinds. It has made good deficiencies in necessities. It has established houses and rooms for recreation. It has been an agent for the dissemination of sound propaganda in camps at home and in the battle area. It has built up the morale in great armies. It has fed families behind the line. It has raised enormous sums of money. It has been a great force for civilization and humanity.

II

THERE are other splendid patriotic organizations, such as the Y. M. C. A., the Knights of Columbus, Salvation Army, Y. W. C. A., Jewish Welfare Board, War Camp Community Service, Camp Activities, and others which have also done yeoman service in many fields.

The days of active field service are practically at an end, as far as our forces are concerned. The Army is home and work in its behalf will soon be reduced to comparatively insignificant proportions. The question arises —what are going to be the peace-time activities of the Red Cross and of the other organizations? Their work must not cease. Millions need their services in this country. Great natural disasters will occur in the future as in the past. It is reasonably certain wars will occur. The Red Cross should be organized and prepared to meet promptly and effectively the demands made upon it.

Our Red Cross must be essentially an American organization if it is to be strong and have the spirit which comes from nationality. It will be called upon from time to time to meet calls for help in various parts of the world. It must be prepared to respond to them in the energetic and generous manner which characterized it in the recent war. To do this it is essential that the organization be maintained upon an effective basis.

III

THE peace-time demands for what we consider normal Red Cross work are a simple problem for the present great organization, with its millions of members; but even these cannot be met effectively unless the organization is continued upon an efficient basis and well-thought-out plans prepared in advance to meet possible emergencies.

The work of the Red Cross during the war has been a wondeful work, beneficial not only to suffering humanity, but helpful and broadening to those who have taken part in it. A wonderful machine has been developed, embodying much of the best ability of our people. Why should we not amplify the field of activity of this and the other great organizations, with their splendid spirit of service, with their millions of enthusastic members and supporters? Why should we not make use of this tremendous force in solving some of our great problems at home?

If we can hold these organizations together, or the greater portion of them, and direct the energies of the splendid men and women who have done so much to help our soldiers, sailors and marines during the war and to aid suffering humanity overseas to bettering the conditions in the slums of our cities, among the poor, and among the industrial workers, results of inestimable value could be attained—results which will make for better relations between capital and labor.

IV

UNITED effort on the part of these organizations for real Americanization, for the establishment of better social and industrial conditions, will deprive the professional agitator of his following and will bring the people from the different walks of life into a more sympathetic understanding and tend to build up that which makes for a Brotherhood of Man. We must go into the highways and byways as have the practical missionaries and organizations of some of our churches and societies; as the Salvation Army has. Americanization and betterment work are not accomplished by the building up of idle organizations, by after-dinner speeches, but by practical work—work which carries with it the human touch. We wish our unassimilated citizens to know what our Constitution and institutions mean; what America stands for. We want them fed on American ideas and ideals and not on the dangerous teachings of a dialect press. We desire them to come under the leadership of Americans and not under that of those who neither understand nor sympathize with our institutions.

The existing spirit of unrest springs in part from conditions which need remedying, in part from vicious and false leadership and in part from the organized dissemination of unsound and dangerous doctrines under the guise of liberal ideas. These conditions can be largely, if not wholly, done away with if the organizations which have done so much during the war attack them with the energy and intelligence with which they attacked the war problems. It is no time now to let these organizations fall to pieces, but rather to redouble their efforts, so that America, strong and united at home, may stand prepared to play her part in the world as we would have her play it.

No Parley with the Reds

I

THERE is room in this country but for one flag, and that is the American flag. Put down the red flag. It stands for nothing which our Government stands for.

It is against everything we have struggled for. It is against the integrity of the family, the State, the Nation. It only floats where cowards are in power. It represents everything we want to avoid.

These are times of dangerous, subversive psychology. The barriers between ordered government and chaos are down in some nations and trembling in others. We must stand squarely on our feet here. Avoid the dangerous doctrines of the hour which are masquerading under the banner of "Liberal Ideas and Progress."

This is no time now for undertaking new theories. The world must once more get on an even keel and settle down after the upheavals of the Great War. It is time now to keep our feet on the ground.

Experience in the training camps brought out very forcibly the desirability of having but one language in our graded public schools, and that language should be the language of the Declaration of Independence, of the Constitution, of Washington, Jefferson, Lincoln, Cleveland and Roosevelt. It is the language of the best democracy.

II

THERE is an element of discontent abroad that is threatening to break down governments and substitute chaos. It is important that we shall be steady, and I can say that in this country 95 per cent of us are steady.

We have no time for the new theory and no desire to listen to too much new preaching. We must keep our eyes on the ground ahead of us and our stride steady, and stand by the Constitution. It has looked at times as if every step we have taken was leading to chaos, but the world will settle down.

We are going to govern this country by Americans and will have law and order. By

Americans I mean men who are living up to the ideals and traditions of the country. The foreigners must be recognized. Through their part in the war they have built up a great spirit of American solidarity. They have stood shoulder to shoulder with us to serve our country. It has been a military age and the war has been of some use. It has given us the flame to fuse the people into a class of Americans. There are problems ahead, but we are going to solve them. All that is needed are two things—courage and common sense. What we want to do is to drive home to these people the meaning of law and the meaning of liberty.

III

THE big issue today is, first and foremost, maintenance of law and order, respect for constituted authority and maintenance of a government under the Constitution.

Ninety-five per cent of American labor is on the square and wants to run straight. Where it is running wrong it is under bad leadership. Give labor American leadership. Don't allow it to drift into the hands of anarchistic Red leaders. As for the Reds, let's stamp them out. They grow only in communities where government is timid and slack. They are a cowardly lot, assassins and murderers often, cowards always. With them go the I. W. W.; their brand is treason.

We've got to follow up our immigrants more closely. Why not instruct them in Americanism? When they get over the gangplank the literature of the Reds is placed in their hands. Let's meet them with the literature of Americanism.

IV

IT seems to me that the watchword today is "steady." We must do all we can to give a square deal to both capital and labor, to push forward good business and increase production. We must also make a much more serious and thorough effort to Americanize the immigrant who comes to us.

I found throughout the disturbances at Gary, at Omaha, and in the coal fields that these aliens were well supplied with the literature of destruction, and that they had barely been touched by Americanizing influences.

The necessity is upon us of promptly getting rid of the alien or naturalized Red either by deportation or proper legal procedure and of emphasizing the vital importance of the maintenance of law and order, respect for property, and the rights of the individual.

The destructive group is small but well organized. The danger from within is not alone from the Reds, but from our own indifference. We must impress upon all these new people, and our own who have become disaffected, that true liberty is found within the law, and never outside it.

v

WE are very proud that America has been called for generations "the refuge of the oppressed." Let us be very careful to see that America doesn't become the dumping ground of the degenerate. What is the use of bringing these people in here who are unfit to be citizens, who are moral degenerates, or descendants of criminals? It isn't enough to be physically sound. I think we must take better care of our immigrant when he arrives. He is met today by the literature of the Reds. His foot is hardly over the gangplank before he begins to receive destructive literature. I think we want to take hold of him, hold on to him for a while, teach him something of our institutions, load him up with good American literature. Let him see what this country really is, have it explained to him, and let us try to arrange, instead of allowing him to settle in racial groups fed by a dialect press in our cities, to influence him or her to go to that section of the country where his or her previous training will be most valuable. In other words, we have got to take hold of our immigration a little more systematically and a little more carefully.

Our Duty to Our Veterans

I

WE sent our men abroad with every possible encouragement, told them how much we thought of them, the splendid mission they were going on, that they were the warriors of civilization, crusaders in a holy cause. We showered upon them everything in the way of praise, encouragement and personal attention. Committees were organized to look after them in camp, to see that they were fed en route to the sea, and to look after them over there. In short, we did everything to send them over in the best possible condition.

They have done the work they were sent to do. They have done it well, done it with sacrifice and great losses. They have fought splendidly, and those who died gave their lives with a smile. Their reckless courage has aroused the admiration of all Europe. They have seen great things, they have felt the spirit of the great adventure, they have seen men die

for an ideal, for duty, for country. They have
worn the uniform with credit, lived up to the
best fighting traditions of our military service, and now they are back, some two millions
of them. No sacrifice has been too great for
them. Losses have not staggered them. In
return, no amount of trouble and care must be
too great for us.

II

IF these men are left to stand in idle groups
they may be misled by the lawless. Neglected,
they will ask themselves, "What were we fighting for? Who are these people for whom we
offered everything and who now forget us?"
We must not fail in our duty to these men.
We have preached patriotism, we have instilled
the spirit of sacrifice, and now is the time to
show that we meant what we said. Don't let
the soldier feel that now that the fighting is
over he is forgotten. Too often that has been
the soldier's fate. We must, in our treatment
of these men, show that we regard the soldier
engaged in righteous war as one discharging
the highest type of citizenship duty.

It is not sufficient to have big public recep-
tions, it is not enough to award medals and

decorations through local communities. All these are good in their way, but we must do something more; we must look after those who need looking after. We must carry out through our local committees a scheme for proper care of the soldier with the same thoroughness with which the Government is attempting to look after the physical and mental restoration of the crippled and unbalanced. . . .

III

IN hospitals, in the convalescent wards and in the streets are small groups of men —men who move slowly or not at all, wrecks of what were once strong, upstanding fellows, who went cheerfully to the front to risk all and give all, if necessary, in the national cause, in the cause of civilization and fair-dealing among nations; men who have given much— limbs, sight, hearing, power of motion, power to do a man's full share in the years to come. We must not forget that they played a man's part and played it greatly for a short but splendid period, and that the obligation is upon us to see that everything humanly possible be done in giving these men such new equipment, such new training for life's work, as the shattered limbs and dulled senses they have left make possible.

They have given greatly for the Nation and for Humanity. Given without stint, without selfishness, without thought of self, and we must labor greatly, plan wisely and provide generously for them, not only as a matter of simple justice to them, but that the youth of the Nation may see that its soldiers are not forgotten; that they may note and remember that a grateful and intelligent people are carrying on to the end, and thereby have the spirit of service strengthened in them.

IV

WITH those who have risked all and given much it is not words and gifts that will count, but rather the protecting care and careful training which will carry on to the end with a purpose single to making them again useful members of society, making them men in whose souls the fires of ambition are once more kindled, men whose sightless eyes see again a light of hope and whose crippled members are once more taught to do the things which will enable their masters to become independent and to feel that they are once more useful members of the community in which they live, that life still holds out much for them. The battle-fields gave them up reluctantly, life came back into their veins slowly, and it remains for us to inspire their souls with hope and confidence in the future.

v

WE must not forget these wrecks of men who went out full of hope, dreaming of gallant deeds, of honor and glad home-comings, looking forward to the family ties which are in the dreams of all normal men. Crippled and shattered, many of them feel themselves hopelessly unfit for life's work, and that they are but wreckage drifting with the tide.

Not only is it important from the standpoint of national morale that we do all possible for these men, but it is most important from that of national economic efficiency.

Success in overcoming the difficulties and the handicaps resulting from wounds often builds up a very real pride of accomplishment and carries one on to greater effort and surprising results—results which at first seemed unattainable and impossible; and out of despondence comes a cheerful, conquering spirit which takes the man over the top again to victory, and in so doing removes many a center of discontent which would draw to itself others.

I

WE hear a great deal about the destructive
work of the soldier. But he also performs a
constructive and life-saving work. Starting
with Porto Rico, we find that, principally due
to the efforts of a medical officer of our Army,
Dr. Bailey K. Ashford, tropical anæmia, or
hookworm disease, as it is ordinarily called,
has been about eliminated. Not only was this
discovery of value in Porto Rico, but it was
made use of throughout our own Southern
States, with a result of revitalizing and re-
energizing hundreds of thousands of people
afflicted with this disease. The annual death-
rate in Porto Rico alone was reduced by a
number exceeding the total number of men
killed during the Spanish-American War, and
a recent inquiry made of all planters in the
island with reference to their workers indicates that, in their opinion, the average increase in efficiency is 60 per cent—a truly

startling figure, and one which illustrates very well the far-reaching and wonderful effects of sanitary measures and preventive medicine.

II

PASSING on to Cuba, here we have the wonderful discovery of Major Walter Reed and his associates, Carroll and Lezear, which resulted in discovering the method of transmission of yellow fever and the means of controlling it, and the eventual elimination of that dread disease not only from Cuba, but from all the American troops, with the resulting saving in life which runs into many thousands each year, and a saving in money so vast that it is difficult to estimate it; for the days of yellow fever, with the consequent quarantine, which tied up the movement of men and materials throughout the entire South, limited the movements of ships coming from yellow fever countries, while costly disinfection resulted in an expenditure running into hundreds of millions. Indeed, it is safe to say that the saving from yellow fever alone every year in life and money has exceeded the cost of the Spanish-American War and the Philippine rebellion.

III

IN the Philippines, splendid sanitary work has been done by the civil government. Beri-beri, one of the most dreaded of the Eastern diseases, has been done away with. Malaria has been brought under control. Infant mortality has been halved. Most of this latter work has been done under the civil government, but the foundations were laid by the medical officers of the Army, who at first had charge of the work. In Panama we see the direct effect of this work in the completion of the Panama Canal. This great and splendid piece of engineering, remarkable as it is from an engineering standpoint, and conducted with wonderful efficiency by General Goethals and his assistants, could not have been built had it not been for the application by General Gorgas of the results of the sanitary discoveries made in Cuba, which made it possible to carry on this great work under conditions of health which equaled those anywhere in the United States. It may be truly said without taking one atom of credit from the engineers that this great work was built on a sanitary foundation. Had we not got rid of yellow

fever and learned to control malaria, the death-
rate would have been so heavy that the work
could only have resulted in our hands as it did
in the hands of the French, for nothing demor-
alizes working forces more effectively than
great epidemics.   They are worse than battles
in some ways.

IV

THE mobilization on the Mexican frontier
was not without its great and lasting benefits.
It enabled us, because of the prevalence of typhoid in the Mexican villages and along the
Rio Grande, to insist upon general typhoid
inoculation of officers and men, and the result
has been the removal of typhoid from the
Army.   When one remembers thousands of
cases in the camps of the Spanish-American
War, the importance of this discovery is appreciated.   The general application was made
possible only by the mobilization of troops and
in the struggle to protect them.   So it was
with the discovery concerning yellow fever
and the elaboration of the methods employed
in controlling malaria.   The results of these
discoveries are now all of general application,
not only to the population in our own coun-

try, but to the population of all countries in and bordering on the American tropics, as well as in the insular possessions. Not only were great sanitary results secured through the military arm of the Government, but it should be remembered also that it, the military arm, established and maintained a civil government in Porto Rico, Cuba and the Philippines, and conducted these governments with great success—in Cuba up to the point of the transfer to the Cuban people of a completely organized republic, and in Porto Rico until the transfer to the American civil government; likewise in the Philippines the military authorities were in full charge during the most trying period and turned over to the civil commission which followed them a well-organized government and a well-filled treasury.

Our Program in a Nutshell

I

THE war is over. The big struggle after the war is on; the struggle of world-wide commerce, and we want to take the proper interest in building up a merchant marine. We want a small but highly efficient army. We want a first-class and ever-ready navy. We want sound public opinion behind some kind of training system. We don't want to see this country ever again fall into such condition of utter helplessness that she cannot immediately become a force to be felt. Verbal massage is a very charming application and quite sedative for a certain length of time. But sometimes we have to demonstrate that force is within us. Sometimes we have to break the peace in order not to break the faith. Sometimes we have to demonstrate that it was the blood of the martyrs which was the seed of the church and not their words.

II

WE hope those times will be few, but sometime they may come, and we must look ahead always to a sound condition of national organization for defense. We don't want in this country, and we won't tolerate for a moment, anything of a militaristic type. What must we do in the matter of the reorganization and establishment of our defense? Whatever we do we are going to do it upon sound American lines, and I think in that purpose we shall have the support of our people throughout the country.

I

GROVER CLEVELAND met issues as
they arose, never shrinking from them. He
realized that in a democracy there must be a
free press, honest criticism, and pitiless pub-
licity; that people must have the facts if they
are to act intelligently. Like Lincoln, he had
absolute confidence in the good sense and judgment of the people once they understood the
issues before them. He realized that without public opinion little could be accomplished.

II

IN the opinion of Grover Cleveland, there
was no room in America for those who were
part American and part something else. Like
Roosevelt, he was intolerant of shams, detested
snobs, and hated insincerity.

With him language was intended to convey

123

ideas and not to confuse the people. He was not an adept at verbal messages. He believed in the Monroe Doctrine absolutely, and in the last words of his inaugural address he said the genius of our institutions forbade any departure from the foreign policy commended by our history, traditions, and prosperity. He rejected the policy of our sharing in foreign broils and ambitions upon other continents, and repelled their intrusion here. He believed in friendship with all nations, entangling alliances with none. He believed in national spirit, and was not a believer in an uncertain, weak internationalism.

III

HE believed in a square deal for labor, in establishing the fullest and best possible understanding and co-operation between labor and capital. He believed in voluntary arbitration of their differences, and to that end he proposed, in his message of April, 1886, that steps be taken looking to the establishment of a Federal settlement of differences between employers and employed. He was also keenly interested in protecting not only the country, but labor, against the inroads of an undesirable immigration.

THEODORE ROOSEVELT

I

AMERICA lost—indeed the world lost—its soundest and most effective advocate of peace when Theodore Roosevelt died. The soundest and most effective because, while hating war, as do most normal men, he realized that the peace of righteousness is often maintained through preparedness—to do our duty even through war, if necessary; and that arbitration is most effective when a nation is not only right, but also able to use force, if needed, to back up the right. He understood that a nation is most effective as a force for peace and for justice when it is of resolute spirit and understands that the strength of right must be organized against the day when it may be necessary to meet the force of wrong.

He understood, as few have, that it is not enough to be filled with the spirit of sacrifice, to have lofty ideals. But that if our sacrifice is to be effective, if our ideals are to be realized, we must have ready the necessary force and organization, moral and physical. To him, empty words and lofty sentiments, unsupported by a resolute and brave spirit and a determination to do one's clear duty, were hateful things, contemptible, dangerous and unworthy of an upstanding and right-thinking people. . . .

II

AS time passes our sense of loss has grown greater and greater, and more and more our people miss the voice which always spoke the truth, the voice whose wisdom and lofty patriotism are more and more understood in these days when we are beset by the temptation to "listen with credulity to the whisperings of fancy," and to "follow with eagerness the phantom of hope"; when the Constitution, which is the foundation of our liberties, and the wise policies which have contributed to our greatness and security are being spoken of as archaic.

III

A CLEAN soul in a vigorous body—this was the impression Theodore Roosevelt made upon me at our first meeting. This first impression never changed, but rather grew as the years went on. We had many tastes in common. We loved the simple and strenuous life, and had that common understanding and appreciation of many things which drew us closely together.

Though a many-sided man, gifted in many ways, his was a simple and open character. He sometimes impressed one as thinking aloud, so frank and unreserved was his conversation. His absolute candor and simple directness were sometimes misunderstood, by those who did not know him, for impetuosity or even egotism, for he spoke of himself as candidly as he did of others, and yet he was, withal, a modest man. He had a keen sense of humor and was quick to see the amusing side of men and events. He was never pessimistic when it was humanly possible not to be. He realized that optimism and pessimism have their roots in the common soil of trouble and uncertainty, and that the one grows up into the sunlight, the other down into the darkness.

His plans grew generally upward and were intended to be seen by a struggling world and to cheer men on.

IV

WHILE he had the simplicity and directness which mark a really great man—one that
has seen enough and done enough to realize
how small he is after all—yet he had great
personal dignity, and could interpose a most
effective barrier against undue familiarity.
He had a wide experience in many fields of
activity, where he had been brought into contact with all sorts and conditions of men, an
experience which had given him a singularly
wide knowledge of human nature and of the
good and weak points of men. He was equally
at home in the mining camp, on the range,
addressing a mothers' meeting, or before the
Sorbonne. This because he was always natural, always himself. While intensely American, his sympathies were as broad as the world.

V

CONSIDERED by some to be rash, im-
patient and intolerant, he was, as a matter of
fact, conservative and patient, especially in a
crisis, always seeking advice from those best
fitted to give it, regardless of party lines or
personal relations. Big enough not to fear

competition or comparison with the best men of the day, he strove to surround himself with the ablest. They were required to be one hundred per cent American, and to have qualifications for the task at hand—nothing more.

He understood the spirit of our people, and they understood him.

VI

HE had a very keen and human interest in that great producer of original wealth, the farmer. He was interested in the building of a merchant marine, and distressed at the absence of our flag on the seas; for in this condition he saw the absence of a merchant fleet in time of peace, with the resulting lack of a naval reserve in time of war, as well as the loss of money paid to foreign shipping for the transport of our products.

As President he pursued an unbroken policy of international understanding and good will. Arbitration took on new life, as the numerous arbitration treaties made while he was President testify.

He did more than any other President to make the world realize what the United States stands for and what "government of the people, by the people, for the people," means to humanity.

His foreign policy was firm and courteous, straightforward and steady, enhancing everywhere respect for American rights and American honor. . . .

In sending the battle fleet around the world he demonstrated that the Pacific is not a closed sea, nor the exclusive zone of influence of any Power.

New life and character were put into our consular service. A Department of Commerce and Labor was created, great desert areas were reclaimed, a wise policy of conservation of our natural wealth was established— one which all far-seeing persons will follow, since it is of vital importance to those who come after us.

VII

AS President his policy was one of preparation, for he understood, as do all who have learned anything from the lessons of history, that a war prepared for is often a war avoided; that it is better to get ready for war and not have it than it is to have war without being ready for it. . . .

In his opinion no man who refuses service to the limit of his physical and mental capacity, when the nation calls, whether in peace or in war, is fit to be a citizen. It was impossible for him to be neutral in the face of wrong.

He dreamed dreams, and he saw visions; he worked hard and played hard; he put his soul into whatever he did.

He was a many-sided man, but four-square to all the world; soldier, statesman, scientist, student of nature, scholar and writer on many subjects, builder of standards, patriot and Christian gentleman — a man whose watchword was Duty, whose guiding stars were Truth and Humanity, whose life was one of service for the right, for country and for GOD.

VIII

IN 1897 he came to Washington as Assistant Secretary of the Navy. He was at the height of his energetic manhood, thirty-eight or thirty-nine years of age, physically hard as nails—a fighter who was beginning to worry the faint-hearted by his demands for vigor in national and international affairs—a keen-visioned and patriotic American who saw storm clouds ahead and realized the need of making ready in advance. In me he found a keen sympathizer, for I had seen enough of Washington to feel that we were rather drifting with the tide in all which pertained to preparedness for possible trouble.

From the very beginning of our acquaintance we were thrown much in each other's company. We were both fond of exercise in the open, and did a great deal of tramping and climbing up and down the banks and cliffs of the Potomac, where it was rough enough to give us a bit of hard work, and took long tramps and runs in such rough country as we could find about Washington.

IX

I WAS then a young medical officer in Washington—on a duty which took me frequently to the White House at all times of night and day. President McKinley, one of the best and most lovable of men, whose real worth and character were too little understood by many, was thoroughly familiar with the views of his Assistant Secretary of the Navy and my own, and he understood and appreciated them. When I came in in the morning he would laughingly ask, "Well, have you and Theodore declared war yet?" and I sometimes replied, "No, Mr. President, we have not, but we think you should take steps in that direction, sir." One night, after we had been talking for some time about the probability of war, the President said with great seriousness, "I shall never sanction war until all efforts to obtain our ends by other means have failed, and only when I am sure that God and man approve. I have been through one great war. I have seen the dead scattered over many battlefields—I have seen the suffering and I do not want to see another unless the cause of right and humanity make it necessary. I pray God we may escape it!" And hesitating a moment, he continued, "But the intolerable situation in Cuba must be terminated, even if it has to be done through war." The President at that time was bearing bravely the heavy burden of serious illness in his family, illness which taxed him to the uttermost, and struggling against a peace-at-any-price group; but rapidly reaching the conclusion that war was inevitable.

x

I OFTEN think, as I look back to those

days, how little the President was understood, for he was really bringing the strongest influences to bear to prepare the country to meet the crisis which was rapidly approaching. In purpose he and his young Assistant Secretary were closer together than either realized at the time. The apparent difference between them was more that of temperament than purpose.

Then came that ghastly report by Senator Proctor, based on his personal observation of conditions then existing in Cuba; conditions of concentration of the starving inhabitants in camps which were death camps; camps of horrors unspeakable—a report which aroused a spirit of hot indignation throughout the Nation and a determination to terminate these conditions. Mr. Roosevelt, John Addison Porter, who was then President McKinley's secretary, and I dined with the Senator at the Metropolitan Club the night before he made his speech, and heard first-hand the substance of what he was to say. We all felt sure that it would result in action on our part, and that the action would be war.

It was about that time that Secretary Long, much exhausted by long, hard service and anxiety, decided to take a short leave. The Colonel and I always took an afternoon run as

soon as he could get out of his office and I
could finish my work. On this particular day
he came up to my house on R Street, panting
hard. He had been running all the way up
Connecticut Avenue. As soon as I came out
on the steps he said: "Leonard, I have done
some real work this afternoon. Mr. Long
went off to take a rest, a much-needed rest."
And with great emphasis—"I was Secretary
of the Navy this afternoon for some three or
four hours, and the responsibility for action
was mine. I have mobilized everything at
Mare Island, at League Island; I have bought
thousands of tons of coal in the Far East for
the fleet; I have directed a certain concentration of ships now in the Far-Eastern waters
under Dewey." Then he stopped a minute
to catch his breath; he said, "You know, I
think Mr. Long will be back in the morning
very early, but I have done what I could to get
the Navy ready."

Next day I asked, "Did Secretary Long
come back?" "Yes," he said, "he was in the
office earlier than he had ever been before, and
it is a question now whether I am sustained
or he. I think the President is going to sus-
tain me." And he did. The young Assistant
Secretary of the Navy, filled with the convic-

tion that war was upon us, and realizing the importance of being ready, unafraid of responsibility, had, in his short period of full authority, done what he deemed best. Subsequent events proved that his action was a wise and far-seeing one, one of far-reaching effect in securing sea control in the Far East and victory in the Philippines.

XI

IN Cuba the Colonel's fine qualities as a leader came out. He was perfectly indifferent to danger, so far as he himself was concerned. He possessed the qualities of an excellent officer. He was ever on the alert in the matter of guarding the lives of his men and looking after their welfare. He never recklessly exposed his men. He was always looking after their interests. He had those fundamental qualities of an officer which lie at the basis of real efficiency—that is, a real interest in the welfare of his men. He was very earnest in their instruction, very careful, very efficient, and very thoughtful of their lives and of their morale. If there was anything short in the regiment and you could not find Colonel Roosevelt, you knew that he was off rustling up something for the men.

During the first fight we were in he was conspicuous for gallantry, always looking after weak points in the line and splendidly cool; nothing whatever of that rather characteristically rapid and impulsive manner, but as well-balanced and cool as an officer ought to be—always on the alert and always ready.

XII

AFTER the fight at Las Guasimas, we had a week of rest before the big fight at San Juan. All of that week he was industriously at work, building up the command in every possible way. Just before the fight I was given command of the brigade and he succeeded me in the regiment. He led the regiment in the attack on San Juan in perfectly splendid fashion. He was cool and collected, and handled his men admirably. In the long days of the siege, after we had taken the heights, he was always on the *qui vive*. I do not remember ever going out along the lines that I did not find Colonel Roosevelt on the alert and where he ought to have been. He was one of the keenest soldiers. He had the same qualities that his sons have shown in France and elsewhere. The Colonel had an inspiring effect upon his men. They almost worshipped

him. He had that rare quality which made his
men feel that they were doing something for
him. There was not a man in the regiment
who did not swear by him. If it was a cook at
a campfire he would stop and say, "Well, you
gave me some pretty good coffee this morning, Brown," or whatever the man's name was.
Always something showing appreciation of the
other man's effort. He had the human touch.

After we had taken Santiago he came back
within a short time with the regiment. You
know the history of the camp at Montauk.

There is no question whatever that if he had
had an opportunity he would have been a military leader of marked distinction—a military
leader fit to handle large forces. He was thoroughly official (if I may use that term) in
military matters. He never presumed upon
acquaintance or friendship. There could not
have been a better disciplined, a more subordinate subordinate than Theodore Roosevelt.

XIII

HE inspired the kind of discipline that was
portrayed by the same old philosopher—the
discipline that comes not from fear but from
respect—respect for the leader and confidence
in him. I do not think any man went through

the Spanish War who had his men more solidly behind him than Theodore Roosevelt, and, I believe, if he had had a chance later on, that he would have gone steadily on, with splendid devotion on the part of his men, and with that growing leadership which would have made him in war the great leader that he was afterwards in the battles of civil life.

I shall always look back to the days which immediately preceded and to those which covered the Spanish War period with the greatest pleasure and satisfaction, for it was then that I learned to love and to understand this man, whose life and work mean so much to America and to the world; whose ideals and policies —if we only live up to them—will be of the greatest value to us today and in the days to come, for he stood for the best and truest Americanism. We never needed him more than we do today.

The sympathy and understanding which were built up in these days continued through his period of service as President, and during the period of the great war. One could not know Theodore Roosevelt without appreciating his rugged honesty, his forgetfulness of self and his absolute devotion to the best interests of this country. One loyalty, one language, one flag, a square deal to all. These were the things he stood for.

XIV

HE was the most inspiring character in our national life since Lincoln. His last message should be stamped upon the heart of all true Americans. He said in part:

"I cannot be with you, and so all I can do is to wish you Godspeed. There must be no sagging back in the fight for Americanism now that the war is over. We should insist that if the immigrant who comes here does in good faith become an American and assimilate himself to us he shall be treated on an exact equality with everyone else. There can be no divided allegiances at all. We have room for but one flag, the American flag, and this excludes the red flag, which symbolizes only war against liberty and civilization. We have room for but one language here, and that is the English language, for we intend to see that the crucible turns our people out as Americans, and not as dwellers in a polyglot boarding-house, and we have room for but one loyalty, and that is loyalty to the American people."